RESHAPING AMERICA

Getting Back *to* Biblical Principles *and the* Fundamental Truths *of* Our Founding Fathers

Curt Flewelling

Edited by Jason Liller and Elliott Bennett.

Cover and text design by Karen Webb.

ISBN: 978-1530180820

For Worldwide Distribution, Printed in the U.S.A.

Dedication

To my beautiful wife.

Table of Contents

Introduction

Barry Loudermilk is a representative in the US Congress from Georgia's 11th district. In 2003, when he was the Republican Party chairman for Bartow County, he traveled to Ukraine where he worked with the Ukrainian Orthodox Church teaching American History, especially the American spirit of liberty and freedom.

One evening, while dining with some government officials, he found himself the center of attention as one of his hosts pressed him for more and more details about the founding of the United States. Impressed with the gentleman's curiosity, Loudermilk finally asked, "Why are you so interested in American History?" The answer, as he put it, changed his life.

"We want to become what you *were.*"[1]

The United States of America is the greatest country in the world. No other nation has risen to such lofty heights so quickly. But, as the Ukrainian official understood, things are changing. We are not what we *were*. Before we embark on a journey to reshape America, we must gain a full appreciation of our country's roots. We need to know who we were as a people. Only then can we fully realize what we have become and, more importantly, what we are fast becoming.

This country was founded on biblical principles—a controversial assertion, yet undeniably true. It would be naïve to think that our greatness was not in large part due to the favor of God. The Ten Commandments are displayed outside of the Supreme Court and many other courthouses for a reason: to remind us of where the laws that govern our lives and our country come from. Man and his principles are ever changing, as we see every day. The principles of our Lord are timeless, inalterable, and true.

Since you're reading this book, chances are you feel as I do: that something is wrong and we need to do something about it. There were three events that got my attention and made me realize that I had to get involved. The first happened in my wife's bible study. She was running late, which wasn't unusual, but this time she had a good reason. The war in Iraq had started and she was sitting in her car, riveted to the first accounts of hostilities.

When she walked into the class, she apologized to the other ladies and told them the reason she was late. An older woman sheepishly put her head down and admitted, "I don't pay much attention to that; it's too upsetting." To me, this was a very odd response. The Iraq War?! How do you not pay attention to that? Furthermore, how do you properly pray for God's protection for everyone involved or affected by this war if you're not paying attention? We are supposed to pray for things like that, aren't we? I realize heavy issues like war are very upsetting (as they should be); however, burying our heads in the sand because it's unpleasant is a recipe for disaster.

The second occurrence happened while watching the news. It was election season and much to my dismay—and I think the Lord's as well—I saw some lunatic politician pounding on a church pulpit and stumping for votes. All of this was done under the guise of "preaching." He railed against various types of social injustices that *his* party could easily cure. Now you and I have seen this phenomenon several times throughout the years but this particular example was strikingly more virulent than others I've seen. Believe it or not, my anger was greater for the deacons, elders, and pastors than it was for the politician. He was just taking advantage of an opportunity; the "leaders" of that church were the ones who let him do it and they should have known better.

Don't get me wrong, I wholeheartedly believe that there is a place to tactfully discuss political issues from the pulpit. However, I also believe that politicians have no business behind a sacred pulpit, especially during campaign season. Before you try to guess the speaker's party affiliation, let me stop you: *it doesn't matter.*

But the trigger that launched me into action took place in my church's parking lot. Several vehicles in the lot had the same bumper sticker endorsing a candidate whose voting record and personal life were very far from biblical principles.

To see bible-believing folks cavalierly check their Christianity at the door and endorse such a person was too much for me. The phenomenon of putting our *spiritual* hats on for forty-eight weeks of the year, replacing it with our *political* hats for four weeks, voting for someone whose belief system has nothing to do with the word of God, and then calmly putting our *spiritual* hats back on after the damage is done, was breathtaking to me! I just wouldn't have it anymore. It was then that I declared "I'm in."

We must approach every aspect of life with the acronym **WWJD** (What Would Jesus Do?) in mind. If we don't, our country will continue to backslide away from God. How can we possibly expect a continuance of His favor? Does Galatians 6:7-8 resonate with anyone? *"Do not be deceived: God cannot be mocked. A man reaps what he sows. Whoever sows to please their flesh, from the flesh will reap destruction; whoever sows to please the Spirit, from the Spirit will reap eternal life."*

Ask yourself: Which of the following most accurately describes me?

CITIZENSHIP SCALE

1. I deeply care about this country. I am intimately aware of the issues of the day and have very developed opinions about them. I am keenly aware of how these issues affect me, my family, my community, and our country as a whole. I attend church regularly, I am active in various community affairs, and I vote regularly.

2. I care about this country. I pay attention to the issues of the day but I don't obsess about them. Some of these issues are important to me but only if they directly affect me, my family, or my local community. I go to church from time to time and only vote in presidential elections.

3. I care about this country but there's not much I can do to affect change. Issues of major importance get my attention but I generally don't have time to watch or listen to the news. I believe in God but only attend church on Christmas and Easter. I don't vote because

there's no difference between Democrats and Republicans; they're all liars.

4. I care about my family. I don't have time to think much about the country and where it's headed. I'm too busy just trying to survive. The only issue of the day I'm concerned about is keeping my job and paying my bills. I don't really think too much about God. I'm not registered to vote.

Thought provoking, huh? Whether you fit into one of these categories or consider yourself an amalgamation of more than one of them, you will get a lot more out of this book if you first carefully reflect upon what type of citizen you are. Your part in reshaping America will be much clearer if you can honestly admit where you are on that scale and, more importantly, where you'd like to be.

This book was born out of a love of God and country. Too many people of faith sat on the sidelines while our country drifted away from its biblical foundation. Sadly, we are no longer drifting; we are careening toward the brink of disaster, and most Christians are not doing much to stop it. Until now, countless people of faith have been content to leave the "heavy lifting" (as it pertains to fighting the various forces that are radically changing the fabric of this country) to our spiritual leaders. Well, our Christian pastors, actors, entertainers, talk show hosts, and TV personalities are tired of fighting this fight alone! Jesus tells his disciples in Matthew 9:37 that *"The harvest is plentiful, but the workers are few."*

Now I realize this verse speaks of leading souls to Christ, but restoring this country to its former greatness requires many workers. That's where you come in. Every long, arduous journey starts with a first step, followed by many more as you do *your* part to

Reshape America. Your friends, co-workers, and others in the community will be watching you and, with God's urging, they will be inspired to do their part as well.

It didn't take a lot of people to get this mighty country off course. The majority of our people either stridently or at least generally believe in biblical principles. If everyone reading this book employed just a few of its suggestions, this nation would be radically changed for the better. Please take the time to prayerfully digest each and every chapter and then ask God what it is you should do to make a change in your community.

I believe the Lord desires a groundswell of believers, motivated by a deep love of God and country, to roll up their sleeves and get to work. Those who believe that this land was not founded on biblical principles and that we must honor the mythical church/state line didn't transform this country by being passive. Christians have sat on their hands far too long and the results are disastrous. I implore you to get in the game. Satan is working overtime to bring us down and, to an extent, he has succeeded. He will not be pleased when God-fearing folks like you rise up. I truly believe that God mourns for the United States and what has become of her. Let's do our part to help restore her to the standing she once had. Let's **Reshape America!**

ACTION STEPS

1. Do some research. Find out if this country was truly founded on biblical principles. Investigate several credible sources including The Declaration of Independence and the Constitution of the Unites States of America.

2. Do some soul searching. Honestly ask yourself, "Where am I on the citizenship scale? Where would I like to be?"

1

The Founding of Our Nation

On July 4, 1776 the American colonies proclaimed that they were free and independent states, no longer subject to English rule. They had suffered enough abuse at the hands of the King. Let's look at the first two paragraphs of The Declaration of Independence so we can get a better understanding of why our nation was founded:

When in the Course of human events, it becomes necessary for one people to dissolve the political bands which have connected them with another, and to assume among the powers of the earth, the separate and equal station to which the Laws of Nature and of Nature's God entitle them, a decent respect to the opinions of mankind requires that they should declare the causes which impel them to separation.

We hold these truths to be self-evident, that all men are created equal, that they are endowed by their Creator with certain unalienable Rights, that among these are Life, Liberty and the pursuit of Happiness. —That to secure these rights, Governments are instituted, among Men, deriving their just powers from the consent of the governed, —That whenever any Form of Government becomes destructive of these ends, it is the Right of the People to alter or to abolish it, and to institute new Government, laying its foundation on such principles and organizing its powers in such form, as to them shall seem most likely to effect their Safety and Happiness.

The uncharted and exhilarating journey upon which the fledging nation was about to embark was bold to say the least. In 1776, nations were basically guided or, more accurately, ruled by tyrannical or quasi-benevolent dictators or despots. A declarative statement by any group demanding input into *how* they were to be governed was unheard of. Furthermore, for this insolent and ungrateful band of misfits to assert that *they* were endowed by their Creator with unalienable rights, and that the king or any other system of government was only as powerful as the governed *allowed* them to be was not only revolutionary but, at the time, absurd. In the Declaration of Independence, the colonists asserted that they were on solid moral ground (God being the arbiter of morality) as they broke away from a government which did not respect their God-given rights. This was a radical departure from the traditional relationship between government and the governed.

OUR FOUNDING FATHERS

Were our Founding Fathers godly men? Some secular scholars will tell you that, for the most part, they were not. At best, they will acknowledge that there were some true Evangelicals, a few more who were Deists, and more who were without religious affiliation. Conversely, other historians, particularly those of faith, will tell you that our Founding Fathers were largely men of faith who drafted our Constitution with God in mind at every turn. So what's the truth? The popular notion that our Founding Fathers were made up of secular men with a few Deists sprinkled in is historically inaccurate.

Before we go any further, let's agree that our Founding Fathers were not perfect men. The discussion of whether this country was founded on biblical principles often never even gets started as folks on the left bring up slavery and folks on the right assert that the Constitution would never have been adopted without provisions that protected slavery. While slavery was, is, and always will be wrong, to assert that these men of faith were not inspired by God is a bit of a stretch. It would be equally disingenuous to assert that the only way this God-inspired document had a chance was to infuse racist provisions into its pages. The admiration we have for these men cannot be one of glorification. More than a few of them were guilty of publicly railing against slavery in the village square while privately perpetuating this abomination at home.

The Founding Fathers from North Carolina, South Carolina, and Georgia were unapologetic slave owners. They never lifted a finger to stop slavery and actually went out of their way to perpetuate it. When someone questions the greatness of these men, they are on pretty solid ground. Others, like Washington, Madison, Franklin, John Jay, and Thomas "All men are created equal" Jefferson owned slaves yet fought relatively hard to abolish slavery. This disconnect is pretty difficult to understand today, and despite their evolution on this issue, I would never attempt to make excuses for them as many historians do. John Adams was the cleanest of the bunch as he fought tirelessly for the abolition of slavery and, like several other founders, never owned a slave.[2] A fair amount of historians scorn some of the Founding Fathers because they were unforgivably inconsistent in their assertion that *all men are created equal* while *owning slaves*. The whitewashing of these historical facts is not helpful, and it gives ammunition to those who castigate our Founding Fathers, often painting them with a very broad brush, asserting that very few, if any, were honorable men and, as a result, the Constitution they drafted is a sham. While I cannot bring myself to call *some* of the Founding Fathers great because of their views on slavery, most of them were men of integrity, and the Constitution which they drafted was a God-inspired masterpiece.

I think we would all be well served to take to heart the words of Bishop Richard Allen, a man born into slavery who founded the first independent African-American church in the United States. He said, "Many of the white people who have been instruments in the hands of God for our good, even such as have held us in captivity, are now pleading our cause with earnestness and zeal."[3] We cannot even begin to reshape America unless we are honest with each other and with ourselves as to who these men were. Let's look at some quotes attributed to our founding fathers:

John Hancock said, "In circumstances as dark as these, it becomes us, as Men and Christians, to reflect that whilst every prudent measure should be taken to ward off the impending judgments... at the same time all confidence must be withheld from the means we use; and reposed only on that God rules in the armies of Heaven, and without His whole blessing, the best human counsels are but foolishness."[4]

James Madison said, "There is no maxim, in my opinion, which is more liable to be misapplied, and which, therefore, more needs elucidation, than the current one, that the interest of the majority is the political standard of right and wrong."[5]

John Adams said, "Suppose a nation in some distant region should take the Bible for their only law book, and every member should regulate his conduct by the precepts there exhibited! Every member would be obliged in conscience, to temperance, frugality, and industry; to justice, kindness, and charity toward his fellow men; and to piety, love and reverence toward Almighty God... What a Utopia, what a Paradise would this region be."[6]

Thomas Jefferson said, "God who gave us life gave us liberty...Can the liberties of a nation be thought secure when we have removed their only firm basis, a conviction in the minds of the people that these liberties are of the gift of God? That they are not to be violated but with his wrath? Indeed, I tremble for my country when I reflect that god is just: that his justice cannot sleep for ever;...a revolution of the wheel of fortune, an exchange of situation, is among possible events: that it may become probable by supernatural interference! The Almighty has no attribute which can take side with us in such a contest."[7]

Benjamin Rush said, "The gospel of Jesus Christ prescribes the wisest rules for just conduct in every situation of life. Happy they who are enabled to obey them in all situations!"[8]

Alexander Hamilton said, "I have carefully examined the evidences of the Christian religion, and if I was sitting as a juror upon its authenticity I would unhesitatingly give my verdict in its favor. I can prove its truth as clearly as any proposition ever submitted to the mind of man."[9]

Patrick Henry said, "This is all the inheritance I can give to my dear family. The religion of Christ can give them one which will make them rich indeed."[10]

John Witherspoon said, "The people in general ought to have regard to the moral character of those whom they invest with authority either in the legislative, executive, or judicial branches."[11]

Samuel Adams said, "And as it is our duty to extend our wishes to the happiness of the great family of man, I conceive we cannot better express ourselves than by humbly supplicating the Supreme Ruler of the world that the rod of tyrants may be broken into pieces, and the oppressed made free; that wars may cease in all the earth, and that the confusions that are and have been among the nations may be overruled by promoting and speedily bringing on that holy and happy period when the kingdom of our Lord and Saviour Jesus Christ may be everywhere established, and all people willingly bow to the scepter of Him who is the Prince of Peace."[12]

Roger Sherman said, "I believe that the souls of believers are at their death made perfectly holy, and immediately taken to glory: that at the end of this world there will be a resurrection of the dead, and a final judgment of all mankind, when the righteous shall be publicly acquitted by Christ the Judge and admitted to everlasting life and glory, and the wicked be sentenced to everlasting punishment."[13]

We would all do well to read The Declaration of Independence and the Constitution of the United States of America. More than a few Americans have never read either of these documents. Most public schools today do a woeful job of teaching from or about them. Given that there is an all-out assault on our Constitution from many factions, the survival of the Republic depends upon citizens who know what these documents mean.

Unfortunately, many of us take the principles of freedom and liberty upon which this country was founded for granted. It is both ironic and sad that those who best understand these principles are often those who have only been in this country a short time. They recall all too vividly from where they came and why they came here in the first place. They are the ones who cry the loudest as they see where this country is going, and they don't need a crystal ball to see how the story ends. Before they even arrived here, they had a very good working understanding of the ideals our Founding Fathers wanted to incorporate into our Constitution almost 250 years ago, and what is at stake if we fail to appreciate and safeguard those ideals today.

ACTION STEPS

1. Read the Declaration of Independence and the Constitution of the United States of America.

2. Research numerous credible sources on our Founding Fathers and the founding of our nation.

3. Ask yourself: What am I doing to challenge our leaders to govern in a constitutional manner?

2

The Separation of Church and State

Most people believe that the phrase "separation of church and state" is in the Constitution. It isn't. Society has a gross misunderstanding of the issue of separation of church and state and this ignorance has led to churches and their pastors being very leery of wading into politically charged waters. If the church is to seize a leadership role in the reshaping of America it's imperative that we all gain a better understanding of how our founders viewed this relationship. Let's start by going back in time to find out what the separation of church and state really means. We must study not only the often misunderstood and, more often, purposely distorted words of Thomas Jefferson; we must also understand the contemporary political landscape.

Thomas Jefferson was elected third President of the United States after an incredibly nasty campaign. The Federalists, who dominated New England and were largely supported by the powerful Congregationalist Church, viciously accused Jefferson of being an atheist. Nonetheless, Jefferson had support in the region from the Baptists which were a religious minority in both size and political power. They were concerned with what they saw as a troubling alliance between the Federalists (the state) and the Congregationalists (religion). They supported Jefferson because he was a proponent of religious liberty.

The Baptists wrote a congratulatory letter to Jefferson praising him for his position. A few months later, Jefferson replied with what is now famously known as the "Letter to the Danbury Baptists." This is the letter that contains the now famous phrase "separation between Church and State." Jefferson's letter to the Baptists was intended to reassure them that he was sympathetic with their beliefs by stating the following: "I contemplate with sovereign reverence that act of the whole American people which declared that their legislature should 'make no law respecting an establishment of religion, or prohibiting the free exercise thereof,' thus building of a wall of separation between Church and State." Anyone at the time, or anyone today, who cares to do a little research would logically conclude that Jefferson was concerned with the "state" encroaching on religious freedoms rather than the "church" aspiring to establish itself as the state. The President then concludes his letter by reciprocating the Baptists' "kind prayers for protection and blessing of the common father and creator of man."[14] Doesn't sound like an atheist to me…

Over the years, "separation of church and state" has morphed into something Jefferson never intended it to mean. I believe Jefferson would have been troubled by how his phrase now seems to guarantee a separation of religious influence from public policy. Rather than look to Jefferson's letter to a group of private citizens, I think we would be better served to take to heart the words contained in the First Amendment of the Constitution: *"Congress shall make no law respecting an establishment of religion, or prohibiting the free exercise thereof; or abridging the freedom of speech, or of the press; or the right of the people peaceably to assemble, and to petition the government for a redress of grievances."* One would think these words are commonly known and understood by the average American, but maybe they're not.

A recent survey by the Newseum Institute found that only 19% of the Americans it polled new that the First Amendment guaranteed freedom of religion. Only 10% of respondents knew that the First Amendment also guarantees freedom of the press. Lastly and most sobering would be the fact that 33% of the respondents had no idea whatsoever what rights the First Amendment guarantees.[15] I guess with numbers like these, it would be wishful thinking to assume that the individuals polled could even remotely understand the church/state relationship. We have our work cut out for us don't we?

The First Amendment says nothing about a "wall" prohibiting the church from encroaching on the state; rather, the amendment prohibits the state from encroaching on the free exercise of religion by its citizens. In the United States, thankfully, religious individuals and the groups with which they affiliate are not bent on establishing a religious entity of any sort that functions as the state. This contrasts wildly with many Muslim countries where Islam *is* the state and vice versa. Our Founding Fathers understood history. They believed that the governed could be trusted far more than a potentially corruptible government.

THE CHURCH

Historically, left-leaning denominations' elder boards and pastors have had very little trepidation discussing politically-charged issues from their pulpits. With little concern for any IRS repercussions (some forms of political speech can and should jeopardize a church's tax exempt status), churches regularly invite politicians to speak about the issues of the day. Coincidentally, these invitations become more frequent during election cycles. Stumping politicians have long courted faith-based voters where they worship, and many left-leaning churches are more than willing to oblige them.

What's interesting is the fact that some of these churches lean to the left doctrinally and far more lean to the left politically. The latter scenario is much more perplexing. If a denomination had a much more liberal view of the Bible (believing some of it, questioning some of it, and flat out disagreeing with the rest of it), then it would make sense for them to rent out their pulpit to a politician who shares those views. However, it is both maddening and confounding to me that good, solid, Bible-believing churches rent their pulpits out to the same left-leaning politicians. Why is this? Simply put, these churches have been sold a bill of goods.

Certain subjects have been hijacked by politicians on the left. An effective way to pull this off is by feigning interest in "social justice," a term we hear a lot these days (and which we'll discuss in more detail in Chapter 4). A fair amount of Bible-believing folks have bought the myth that conservatives are compassionless, greedy jerks who don't care about the poor. These congregants are swayed by politicians who stump for votes from behind the pulpit by painting their opponent or opponent's party as heartless. They offer simple solutions for complex problems by simply telling congregants that their redistributive policies are helpful to the poor.

There are politicians at the highest level who advocate that Jesus is down with such policies. It takes a lot of nerve and a fair amount of biblical ignorance to believe such a concept. These folks and their constituents are either unfamiliar with or unwilling to ponder Paul's words to the Thessalonian church in 2 Thessalonians 3:10: *"For even when we were with you, we gave you this rule: 'The one who is unwilling to work shall not eat.'"* State-sanctioned redistribution of wealth doesn't change hearts. Rather, it has the opposite effect as it often embitters people toward the very ones whom God wants us to help. 1 John 3:17 says, *"If anyone has material possessions and sees his brother in need but has no pity on him, how can the love of God be in him?"*

A government that is generally indifferent and even increasingly hostile toward God can hardly be the entity to ensure that God's love is in anyone. It's God's job first and foremost to put that love in a person's heart. Secondly, it is up to the individual to cultivate and then express a willingness to show that love to others. Any urging to express that love is best done by God rather the state. I believe Jesus is much more concerned with the hearts of individuals rather than the collective of our citizenry.

If a wealthy man who lives in a large house on the hill is *compelled by the state* to help the poor man who lives in a van down by the river, how much has the wealthy man's heart really changed? Although our government does have an obligation to help the less fortunate, I believe that God has something grander in mind. If a church espouses true biblical principles, then its individual congregants, and the church as a whole, will give to the less fortunate out of Christlike love and compassion rather than government edict.

The former brings us closer to Christ while the latter may even stir up unchristian feelings like anger and resentment. Yet despite this simple premise, Bible-believing folks often offer up a hearty "A-MEN" to a politician who tells them that they want the government to do more to help the poor. Historically, the poor have been helped in many ways by the church and by Christians in general with very little government intervention. Mission trips, food pantries, clothing drives, urban renewal projects, community recreation centers, athletic programs, and summer camps are all examples of community outreach which the church has traditionally spearheaded.

Perverting a term like "social justice" in order to divert attention away from a politician's record on other issues is, for lack of better words, absolutely pathetic. Sadly, it's also an effective tactic. If Bible-believing folks simply focused on a politician's voting record/personal life as it pertained to issues such as abortion, same-sex marriage, marital infidelity, stem cell research, welfare reform, gambling, and the death penalty, to name a few, they would never allow certain candidates to stump for votes from their church's sacred pulpit.

Congregants should know better than to tolerate this type of nonsense in their churches around election time. Pastors and elder boards should *really* know better, as their understanding of where Jesus stands on the issues should be even greater than their congregants'. With this knowledge in mind, they should be ashamed of themselves for their decision to whore out their pulpits to political opportunists. Churches have an obligation to educate their congregants on the **entire** Word of God and not merely focus on, or in some cases even contort, the Word.

CAN WE BE ARRESTED FOR OUR FAITH?

Sadly, yes. Until recently, religious persecution has been a phenomenon that has mainly occurred in other parts of the world. We, as a nation, pride ourselves in the fact that we are religiously tolerant. Unfortunately, that is no longer accurate. We are still a relatively tolerant nation when it comes to most faiths, but when it comes to Christianity, it's a different story. Jesus said, in John

15:18-19, "*If the world hates you, keep in mind that it hated me first. If you belonged to the world, it would love you as its own.*" Since there is only one way to heaven, Jesus Christ, we worship the one ***true*** God. Logically, this means that all other gods are false. Therefore, society, without even realizing it, is going to be more tolerant of false gods and their followers than the true God and His followers. This is in keeping with what Jesus said in John 15.

The tenets and precepts of most religions are no threat to political parties or of a truly civil and orderly society. Therefore, they can be placated and even accepted without much fanfare, but Christianity espouses many things that offend a lot of people. Since most Americans think we live in a democracy rather than a representative republic, mob rule sometimes rears its ugly head when politicians fail to lead, instead giving in to the demands of their constituents. The result is that godly rhetoric espoused by godly men under the protection of the Constitution becomes "hate speech" simply because some citizens think that the biblical principles upon which this country was founded are archaic and irrelevant in today's world.

Thoughtful pastors understand that biblical principles don't bend and swerve to accommodate man. Just because our culture's views operate on a sliding scale, that does not mean pastors or citizens should check their beliefs at the door when it comes to public discourse. To do this would be the tail wagging the dog. God created this world, and He told us how to live. As ambassadors of Christ, we have a duty to represent Him and His principles at every turn.

This country was founded by men who fought hard to get away from religious persecution. Since biblical times, a staggering number of countries have viewed the simple exercise of religious belief as a serious threat to the state. America was a glorious experiment whereby, for the first time in human history, the people (in the form of a representative republic) determined what was in their best interest. The free exercise of religious expression was at the cornerstone of this experiment. It would be naïve to think that a crackdown by the state would not eventually come to this country.

Indeed, what has sadly been happening around the world for centuries is now here. What started in the form of pseudo congregants secretly monitoring what was being preached in our churches has become much more heavy-handed. Not since the days of King George III has there been such a blatant attempt to extinguish free religious expression. Where has this travesty taken place? Hawaii? California? Washington? How about Texas?

Houston Mayor Annise Parker, who is openly gay, demanded that five pastors in her city hand their sermons over to the government.[16] These sermons included opposition to Houston's Equal Rights Ordinance, which the pastors believed would have several unintended consequences, such as allowing transgender men to use women's restrooms. Opponents of the ordinance generated more than 50,000 signatures in order to put a referendum on the ballot opposing it. Although only 17,269 signatures were needed to get the referendum on the ballot, the City of Houston rejected the petition over alleged irregularities. The opponents of the ordinance filed a lawsuit against the city.

Houston countered by issuing subpoenas to local pastors which demanded their sermons on the subject. This move goes way past bullying; it is tyranny. As is often the case, the powers that be grossly underestimated the pushback that followed. As plans to send Mayor Parker thousands of sermons and bibles from around the country were about to unfold, the mayor started to feel the heat.

The city attempted to placate opponents of their Orwellian demand by changing the verbiage in the subpoena to read "speeches" rather than "sermons," thinking it may throw the hounds off the scent—an illustration of colossal ignorance as it pertains to free speech. Free speech is free speech whether it is religious in nature or not. No one was fooled. Facing growing opposition culminating in an "I Stand Sunday" event to unify multiple groups opposed to this infringement on free speech, the mayor backed down and withdrew the subpoenas. What an inspiring example of concerned citizens rising up and taking a stand against tyranny!

Whether Mayor Parker was naïve or merely floating a trial balloon is irrelevant, as opponents of religious liberty will keep trying until Jesus returns. The Houston showdown brings up a good question: "Do we have the right to say whatever we want as long as we think we have the Scripture to back it up?" No. Take for example the contemptible "Christians" of Westboro Baptist Church. Their vile rhetoric and insensitive actions toward homosexuals and their practices do not even remotely display the love of Christ, and they will be judged harshly for what they have done in God's name. The reason you and I have such a difficult time conveying to a lost world that Christians hate sin but love sinners is because of lunatics such as these. Elliott Bennett put it best when he said, "The God we serve is not the people who serve him."

In its quest for this profoundly misunderstood concept of "the separation of church and state," government entities both small and large are clamping down hard on religious freedoms in America. Things that used to only happen in totalitarian regimes are now happening in our own country under the guise of the separation of church and state.

When you define the verbiage, you win the war. One of the more disturbing tactics that government entities in America are starting to employ is to label biblical truths as "hate speech." This trend logically has no bounds as "the state" becomes increasingly dismissive and hostile toward the Word of God. As Pastor Jeff Shreve rightly stated, "The Bible is an offensive book."

Of course we as believers understand what Pastor Shreve means, but too many people do not. Rather than viewing the Bible as an instruction manual for life, these people find it a judgmental book that simply makes people feel bad about who they are or what they engage in. In their minds, the preaching of this hate-filled book has to be curtailed, and they are attempting to do this by hate speech legislation all across the land. When a government wants to silence someone, they can simply brand their rhetoric as hateful and legally shut them up. *When you define the verbiage you win the war.* To define true, timeless and inerrant principles which are espoused *in the Bible* as "hate speech" is to create hate speech toward Christians and anyone else who believes in biblical principles.

The attitude of those pastors in Houston is one we all should adopt as Christians. To sum up their philosophy, let's go to Acts 5:27-29: *"The apostles were brought in and made to appear before the Sanhedrin to be questioned by the high priest. We gave you strict orders not to teach in this name, he said. "Yet you have filled Jerusalem with your teaching and are determined to make us guilty of this man's blood." Peter and the other apostles replied: "We must obey God rather than human beings!*

THE STATE

A chilling example of obeying God and paying dearly for it is the saga of Iranian American Pastor Saeed Abedini. Pastor Abedini converted to Christianity in 2000, which is punishable by death in many Islamic countries. For nine years he spread the word of God in an Islamic state while not doing anything illegal, a challenging endeavor to say the least. His work with "house churches" was becoming more troubling to the government and in 2009 he was detained and told to cease his work with the house (underground) churches and was "encouraged to do only humanitarian" work. In 2012 he returned to Iran to work on a government-approved project to build orphanages. While visiting his parents, he was detained again and placed under house arrest. His passport was confiscated by the Iranian Revolutionary Guard and he was forbidden to leave the country.

He was eventually charged with undermining national security, although the government's specific allegations against him were never made public. Pastor Abedini told the government that he would not do anything illegal, but also wouldn't stop standing up for his beliefs. Those beliefs led a judge to sentence him to eight years in Evin Prison, a fate reserved for individuals who the government sees as a threat and would like to break both mentally and physically. Pastor Abedini has endured psychological and physical torture at the hands of his captors throughout his first two years in prison.

Even though our government is increasingly hostile toward people of faith (almost exclusively Christians), we do not yet throw our citizens in jail for exercising their religious beliefs. However, we are throwing the founding principles of this nation away at an alarmingly rapid pace. As I've noted, our government was unlike any government ever formed, and its three branches were set up to *protect and uphold the God-given* rights of its citizens. In the last few decades, the three branches of government have not only failed to do this, but they have sought to replace these God-given rights with *government*-given rights. The government simply cannot and should not attempt to do what only God can do.

The danger in this is obvious; God-given rights cannot be taken away by man, government-given rights can. A society is only as free as its government will allow it to be. If that government has a fundamental understanding and respect for a constitution founded on God-given rights, they'll be okay. If a government doesn't understand nor respect this premise, we're gonna have some problems. The latter scenario will result in the United States being no different than any other country.

A notable common denominator of totalitarian, freedom-squelching regimes is their penchant for eradicating God from the landscape. There are many reasons that these forms of government seek to prohibit their citizens from free worship. A belief in God (even a false god) stirs an individual to hope. If the state is to be all-powerful, its citizens must be dispirited, not hopeful. Their foolish worship of an invisible god must be extinguished, lest they derive any comfort other than that which is beneficently piecemealed out by the state. For any totalitarian regime to thrive, its citizens must look to *it*, not to God, for its sustenance. Let's look at how history's most infamous statists viewed religious influence on the formation of their totalitarian regimes:

Martin Bormann, Nazi leader, said: "National Socialism and Christian concepts are incompatible."[17]

Joseph Goebbels, Nazi Minister of Propaganda, said: "The National Church demands immediate cessation of the publishing and dissemination of the Bible in Germany."[18]

Joseph Stalin said: "You know they are fooling us, there is no God, all this talk about God is sheer nonsense."[19]

Karl Marx said: "Communism begins where Atheism begins," and "The first requisite for the happiness of the people is the abolition of religion." Marx also said, "Atheism is a natural and inseparable part of Marxism."[20]

Vladimir Lenin said: "It is true that liberty is precious, so precious that it must be carefully rationed," and "Give me four years to teach the children and the seed I have sown will never be uprooted."[21]

These men all knew how dangerous liberty and freedom were to the designs of an all-powerful state. A citizen's right to political dissent or, even worse, to worship any god other than the god that is the state was intolerable. This freedom would be even worse if the god the citizenry chose to worship espoused beliefs that were in direct conflict with that state. Let's contrast the ideologies of these brutal, godless men with the ideology of one this country's most recent leaders, Ronald Reagan. Reagan said, "Freedom prospers when religion is vibrant and the rule of law under God is acknowledged." He also said, "Within the covers of the Bible are the answers for all the problems men face."[22]

Reagan had a long history of fighting Communism before he ever became a politician, so when he became president, he wasted no time calling the Soviet Union the "Evil Empire." Communist regimes all over the world despised him for this, as they knew he loved liberty and freedom. The leaders of these regimes intuitively knew that these concepts were kryptonite to totalitarianism, and they hated him for having the courage to identify evil when he saw it.

Isaiah 9:6 says, *For to us a child is born, to us a son is given, and the government will be on his shoulders. And he will be called Wonderful Counselor, Mighty God, Everlasting Father, Prince of Peace."*

What does "the government will be upon his shoulders" mean? It simply means that everyone and everything is subject to the Lord Jesus Christ and his principles. The President of Lane Theological Seminary, Lyman Beecher, put it this way:

> *The government of God is the only government which will hold society, against depravity within and temptation without; and this it must do by the force of its own law written upon the heart. That is that unity of the Spirit and that bond of peace which can alone perpetuate national purity and tranquility—that law of universal and impartial love by which alone nations can be kept back from ruin. There is no safety for republics but in self-government, under the influence of a holy heart, swayed by the government of God.*[23]

Through the ages, the best governmental intentions and principles that man could come up with have always been pitifully woeful in comparison to God-breathed principles. Our governmental system is unique in the respect that it is founded on Judeo-Christian principles. Formulating these God-inspired principles into a governmental system is essential to the formation of any enduring republic. However, if the representatives of that republic and its constituency are not willing to allow their hearts to be swayed by God, we have arrived at the beginning of the end. Our unique and extraordinary system has worked wonderfully for nearly 250 years precisely because our leaders and their constituents have submitted their wills and opened their hearts to God's will for our country.

Do enough of us even care enough about this country to employ all or any of the principles set forth in this book? Obviously you do because you are taking the time to read it. However, many of us take for granted the freedoms and liberties our forefathers fought and died for. Most of us seemed to get stirred or whipped up in a patriotic fervor during times of national crisis such as World War I, World War II, or the 9/11 attacks. However, this enthusiasm doesn't seem to last for most of us. We slip back into our daily routines with the notion that, since we live in America, "We'll be fine. It's always gonna somehow work out." Heretofore, it always has eventually "worked out" because of two very distinct reasons: first, we are predominately a Christian nation and we have always found great favor with God; and second, God-fearing, hardworking Americans have never forgotten what we were breaking away from, what ideals and principles we wanted to establish, and who sustained us during the wobbly beginnings of our nation.

During one of those times of crisis, World War II, Congress saw fit to include the Pledge to the Flag in the United States Flag Code. This was the first official sanction of the pledge since its creation some fifty years prior. The Pledge of Allegiance was first created in 1892 as a celebratory remark used throughout public schools in celebration of the 400th anniversary of Columbus's discovery of the New World. Despite the fact that the pledge had been widely recited by teachers and school children at the start of their day, and by common citizens at a wide array of public events, it was not until June 22, 1942 that it was officially sanctioned. In 1945, the pledge received its official title: The Pledge of Allegiance. In 1954, President Dwight D. Eisenhower gave the pledge its current form by adding the phrase "under God" in order to differentiate the United States from the officially atheist Soviet Union: *"I pledge Allegiance to the Flag of the United States of America, and to the Republic for which it stands: one Nation under God, indivisible, with Liberty and Justice for all."*

As President Eisenhower authorized this change, he said, "In this way we are reaffirming the transcendence of religious faith in America's heritage and future; in this way we shall constantly strengthen those spiritual weapons which forever will be our country's most powerful resource in peace and war."[24] Presidents since Eisenhower have also noted that America is a God-fearing nation and have been maligned for their assertions. President Ronald Reagan was soundly chastised by the left when he referred to the former Soviet Union as the "Evil Empire." Some years later, George W. Bush was similarly criticized for calling Iraq, Iran, and North Korea the "Axis of Evil." What do these nations have in common? They are either officially godless or officially worship a god other than the God of Israel. Although the pledge does not specifically refer to the God of Israel, the influence the true God of Abraham, Isaac, and Jacob had and has on this nation is irrefutable.

In a world that seems to be rapidly spinning out of control, I find it charmingly old-fashioned that many of our children still recite the pledge in our schools. It's a constant reminder to youngsters of who we are, whom we serve, and what we stand for. In general, I think it's a pretty good idea for all of us to believe wholeheartedly in the principles espoused in the Pledge of Allegiance. However, please don't misinterpret my opinion of one's willingness to "pledge allegiance" to a state or representation of that state (the flag) as an endorsement of any form of unwaveringly blind nationalism. My endorsement of reciting the Pledge of Allegiance has almost everything to do with the fact that the pledge acknowledges that we are a nation *under* God that believes in liberty and justice for all. If the government of this nation ever officially changes this oath of loyalty to declare that we are no longer a nation under God and are ambivalent or hostile toward the concepts of liberty and justice, I can no longer endorse such a pledge and you shouldn't either.

As citizens, what should our relationship with the United States government look like? For some guidance, let's look at Romans 13:1-2: *"Let everyone be subject to the governing authorities, for there is no authority except that which God has established. The authorities that exist have been established by God. Consequently, whoever rebels against the authority is rebelling against what God has instituted, and those who do so will bring judgment on themselves."* To some, these verses pretty much say "like it or not, we have to obey the government and short of voting governmental officials out, there's not a lot we as citizens can do." Many with this philosophy contend that religion and politics are two very separate entities which, under our Constitution, can't intersect.

These individuals do their "religion" thing over here and their "political" thing over there. This philosophy is also held by individuals who are not even remotely inclined to look up, let alone care about, Romans 13: 1-2. These individuals believe in the separation of church and state, and although they are generally irreligious, they often find themselves agreeing with so-called "Christians" who think the mingling of religion and politics is not a good thing.

Another category of individuals are of the mindset that most governments are generally corrupt and we have every right to resist them when they are out of line. To understand what Paul was trying to convey, I think we have to define the word "rebel": "To refuse allegiance to and oppose by force an established government or ruling authority"[25] If we are going to have any chance of obeying God's word in this area, we are going to have to shift our focus from government officials to the government in general. Government, as Paul was referring to it, was supposed to be a *good* thing. Romans 13:3-4 says:

For rulers hold no terror for those who do right, but for those who do wrong. Do you want to be free from fear of the one in authority? Then do what is right and you will be commended. For the one in authority is God's servant for your good. But if you do wrong, be afraid, for rulers do not bear the sword for no reason. They are God's servants, agents of wrath to bring punishment on the wrongdoer.

Originally, and presumably today as well, government is supposed to protect its citizenry from harm, but this only works if the government is set up to respect God, the arbiter of right and wrong. That's why the original intent of our forefathers was to set up a government based on Judeo-Christian values, in essence shaping our laws with the ultimate judge, God, at the core. When God gets further and further from the equation, the original intent of government becomes perverted. Once this perversion becomes egregious, God's directive to submit to government becomes subordinate to our first allegiance, which is to God.

Honoring government to the exclusion of common sense is beyond foolish. When a government is largely made up of officials who have no moral compass and who blindly follow equally godless constituents rather than leading them, disaster is imminent. Notice I used the word "blindly." Tyrannical governments do not emerge overnight. They evolve when moral, decent, God-fearing folks simply sit on their hands. Jesus didn't shy away from action and neither should we.

At what point do we say "enough is enough?" when it comes to perpetual acquiescence to the state? It is my belief that although the United States Government has lost its way in terms of governing or legislating in a godly manner, we should still submit to their authority. Many in our citizenry are fooled by these individuals, but God is fully aware of what is in their hearts: vengeance is His.

Very few individuals are up for rebellion. Paying attention to the issues of the day and trying to change our government via a peaceful grassroots effort is always preferable to violent rebellion.

So you see, submitting to a government that is supposed to uphold good makes sense. However, blindly submitting to a government that upholds evil is not only foolish, but is contrary to God's will. The ultimate result of blindly following such entities is clearly laid out for us from the beginning of time. In every case, when a government becomes unmoored and drifts from Godly governance, the results are disastrous.

The conundrum that faith based organizations face is how to promote their principles in the political arena without jeopardizing their 501-(c)(3) or (4) statuses. According to the Internal Revenue Code, a 501-(c)(3) or 501-(c)(4) is a non-profit organization that is exempt from paying federal income tax. A 501-(c)(3) organization is a public charity, private foundation or private operating foundation, with open membership. A 501-(c)(4) organization is a civic league or association operated exclusively for the promotion of social welfare or local associations of employees with limited membership.[26, 27]

Ironically, you can't, in good faith, enjoy tax-exempt status by being a "religious" organization and then turn around and cry foul when the federal government wants to inquire about what your business practices happen to be as they pertain to politics. However, this is not to say that a government, or more specifically, a government entity such as the IRS, can unfairly and disproportionately target Christian and conservative groups solely based upon their ideology. This is precisely what happened between 2010 and 2012 when the IRS exclusively targeted such groups for protracted and unfair scrutiny when processing their 501(c)(3) applications.

RESHAPING AMERICA

The results of the 2010 midterm elections yielded historically large victories for conservatives nationwide. Many members of the government did not want a repeat performance of this in 2012. This fear spawned a concerted effort by the IRS to subject these groups to long and unreasonable examinations which, in many instances, rendered them ineffective for those years leading up to the 2012 general election. Even though the treatment of Christian/Conservative groups during this period was wrong, we must not confuse or intentionally blur the facts when complaining about governmental inquiries into religious/conservative groups. Asking legitimate questions about their ideologies and methods of operation are certainly permissible.

As a "religious" organization, you can't have your cake and eat it too. As a church you do have the right to host political debates, pass out voter guides that detail the prospective candidates' stands, and discuss the current events from the pulpit. However a church cannot overtly promote specific candidates, an activity that is clearly inappropriate for an organization that benefits from tax-exempt status. Pastors who feel that their First Amendment right to free speech is violated by these restrictions are simply wrong. The sad thing is that a thoughtful pastor can do all the aforementioned things that he is permitted to do and get his political point across loud and clear without jeopardizing his church's tax-exemption.

The beginning of the end of any government or nation comes when God is trivialized, marginalized, and ultimately eliminated. Totalitarian regimes always stamp out God as their first order of business. When God is slowly but surely crowded out of a society, something will replace Him. Often it's an immoral, evil, and brutal government. The state becomes Mommy, Daddy, and ultimately God, while many righteous individuals step back and say

"How did this happen?" If we aren't careful, it will happen to us. Actually, in many facets of life, it's already begun.

ACTION STEPS

1. Read Amendment I to the Constitution of the United States of America.

2. Research what you and your church are legally permitted to do in the area of politics.

3. Ask your pastor what your church is doing to affect change in today's culture.

3

Politics

The days of looking at politics as a Republican or Democratic thing are long gone. Depending upon where you live, you will find conservative Democrats and liberal Republicans. Although these parties do have platforms which articulate something of an ideology, they can be a little misleading, often replete with platitudinous generalities designed to entice some to remain in or join the party while not offending other potential converts or current party members.

Some politicians agree wholeheartedly with their party's platform, some assert that the platform is too extreme, while others contend that it's not bold enough. For these and many other reasons, the days of voting for a straight party ticket should be over. They unfortunately are not. Doing your due diligence in thoughtful analysis of a potential candidate is just too time-consuming for some voters. It's much easier, and lazier, to view a few political ads a few weeks before an election and then make an uninformed, emotional decision based on the false notion that this party is for one thing and that party is for another. It's more complicated than that.

As troubling as this phenomenon is, there are even worse reasons to pledge unwavering party loyalty. Many voters cast their ballot for a Democrat or Republican knowing full well that they are voting for a party hack rather than a leader. These individuals are neither altruistically hopeful nor naïve when it comes to backing candidates. They vote for people who will say or do anything in order to win. The (R) or (D) becomes more important than right or wrong. It's a big game to these folks.

Charlie Crist of Florida is a walking, talking example of this phenomenon. In November 2014, Charlie Crist narrowly lost to Governor Rick Scott in a hotly contested gubernatorial race. Governor Scott turned the State of Florida around in many areas, and, for the most part, did a very good job. So why was he in danger of losing his governor's seat? What does Charlie Crist bring to the table that is so attractive to half of Florida's registered voters? Unfortunately, Mr. Crist's biggest asset is his willingness to be anything he needs to be in order to get elected.

As pathetically sad as this character trait is, it is very useful when a large percentage of voters simply vote for the (R) or the (D). Mr. Crist is a Democrat (at least he is today). Why do I add that? Because Charlie Crist's epiphanies over the last few years have come fast and furious. I urge Floridians not to blink as Charlie Crist may soon re-invent himself again should he find it necessary to do so. In the span of twelve short years, he has become the quintessential poster boy for political expediency. As a Florida state senator, Crist billed himself as a pro-life, pro-traditional marriage, Reagan conservative. He voted conservatively and even publicly called for the resignation of President Clinton during the Monica Lewinsky scandal. As Governor, Mr. Crist was at best a liberal Republican. He had aspirations of becoming the

Republican Party's nominee in the 2008 Florida senate race, but he trailed in the polls to the eventual winner, Marco Rubio.

Rather than face a primary defeat, Mr. Crist became an independent. After losing his senatorial bid, one would hope Mr. Crist would become somewhat introspective. After all, falling from the perch of promising conservative state senator to a widely criticized liberal Republican governor and ultimately ending up a defeated independent senate candidate can't be easy. So what was Mr. Crist's next move? For a man with such malleable ideals as Charlie Crist, the choice was obvious.

Charlie Crist became a personal injury lawyer. Talk about going from the frying pan to the fire! Not content chasing ambulances, Mr. Crist did the only thing he knew how to do: re-invent himself. And re-invent himself he did. Crist emerged as a pro-choice, pro-gay marriage, liberal Democrat candidate in the 2014 Florida governor's race. In a sick and ironic twist, Hillary Clinton, scorned wife of the man Charlie Crist admonished twelve years prior, actively campaigned for him.[28] You just can't make this stuff up!

To me, if you are a Christian, your job as a voter is infinitely easier, as you have a template to use as your voting guide: The Bible. However, you still have to analyze previous voting records as well as personal and professional conduct (particularly if an individual is a newcomer to politics) when choosing a candidate. Unfortunately, most politicians of either party will say or do just about anything to get elected. You cannot automatically assume that one's party affiliation guarantees that they will legislate or govern in a more biblical manner than their opponent.

There was a time when I felt the Republican Party was a safer bet on faith-based issues, but now I'm not so sure. The ever-evolving, rudderless Republican Party that we know today has caused many potential voters to register as independents. Heretofore, an independent was someone who wasn't actually sure where they stood on many issues, or found themselves sometimes agreeing with Democrats, sometimes with Republicans. However, this ever-increasing new breed finds itself disagreeing with both parties much of the time. They simply do not want to affiliate with parties that stand for nothing yet will say anything to get elected.

What about Libertarians or independents with a libertarian bent? The option to become a Libertarian or vote for Libertarian candidates is very appealing in these trying times. The *American Heritage Dictionary* defines a Libertarian as "One who believes in freedom of action and thought; one who believes in free will." During these times when our federal government massively encroaches on virtually every aspect of our lives, the thought of a Libertarian candidate in the White House or Congress is appealing. The very religious freedoms we as Christians enjoy are impossible in a governmental system that doesn't respect such principles. Although many principles of the libertarian thought process are indeed appealing to the faith-based voter, some are not.

We as Christians do not serve a God who is okay with a woman's right to "choose," particularly if she chooses abortion. We as Christians do not serve a God who is okay with legalizing drugs that can radically alter a person's frame of mind and kill their motivation. 2 Timothy 1:7 (NKJV) says *"For God has not given us a spirit of fear, but of power and of love and of a sound mind."* We as Christians do not serve a God who is okay with anything and everything people do, just as long as it's in the privacy of their own homes. Ecclesiastes 12:14 says: *"For God will bring every deed into judgment, including every hidden thing, whether it's good or evil."* Given the "live and let live" philosophies of the Libertarian, do we as Christians summarily dismiss Libertarians or libertarian thought? The answer is no.

As previously stated we would not be able to openly worship the God of Israel would it not be for the freedoms that Libertarians doggedly defend. However, as an orderly and civilized country whose principles and laws were founded on Judeo-Christian principles, we must insist on a government that protects and serves us in a manner that is consistent with biblical principles. Christians don't worship man, we worship God, and God is not down with many of the ideals espoused by Libertarians. It's a sad reality that many brilliant thinkers and visionaries always seem to miss the most glaringly obvious principles. Their brains grasp complex concepts while missing basic ones. Such is the mind of many Libertarians. They have an incredibly clear understanding of liberty and freedom while failing to understand that the ultimate giver of these things is God.

Let's look at the Christian right. The Christian left (oh yes, there is a Christian left) would describe the Christian right as mean spirited, homophobic, angry, intolerant, and puritanical. Some on the Christian right might rebut those characterizations in the following manner:

We are not mean spirited; we merely try to point out the truth in a passionate way, and it's your problem if the truth hurts. We are not homophobic; we are simply fed up with the pro-gay agenda and will do everything in our power to stop it. As far as painting us as angry, well you got that one right. We are angry! Jesus was righteously indignant when he confronted sin, and we should be too. We are not intolerant; we are welcoming to a point, but we must never tolerate sinful behavior. Puritanical means "very strict in moral or religious matters, often excessively so; rigidly austere." I don't think that describes us. I can understand how someone who does not subscribe to the Bible as their rule book would view these Christian principles as excessive, but the fact of the matter is that we (well, most of us) are not as uptight as non-believers think we are.

I know a fair amount of folks on the Christian right who are not mean spirited, but I also know a fair amount who are. Whether folks on the Christian right are mean spirited or are only perceived as mean spirited, the result is the same. Some on the Christian right have become very frustrated with all the branches of local, state, and federal government, the media, the entertainment industry, and their "worldly" brethren as they see the world going to Hell in a hand basket. Lashing out against this or that social ill can look mean spirited, even when it's not. Christ hates sin but never admonished anyone in a mean-spirited way. Nor should we. Believe it or not, we can be righteously indignant and not be mean spirited. Is this tough to pull off? Absolutely. However we must do it in order to develop relationships with un-churched individuals with the hopes that they will eventually be receptive to the gospel.

The world is increasingly full of thin-skinned individuals who see *any* attempt to comment on cultural issues from a biblical perspective as mean spirited. A healthy cognizance of this hypersensitivity is in order. As 1 John 4:11 says, *"Dear friends, since God so loved us, we also ought to love one another."* If we first possess this love, our concern for how far adrift someone may be is more likely to be met with openness rather than hostility. Sin is combated one person at a time. Your fellow citizen is going to perceive you as holier-than-thou if he doesn't first feel loved.

VOTING

At this point you're probably asking yourself, "Who *do* I vote for?!" Although everyone has to ultimately make this decision on their own, we all have a great reference book to help us out: The Bible. A good place to start would be to meditate on Psalm 111:10, which says: *"The fear of the Lord is the beginning of wisdom; all who follow his precepts have good understanding. To him belongs eternal praise."* If we seek God's perspective on everything, not just whom to vote for, we will never go wrong. Proverbs 3:5-6 says: *"Trust in the Lord with all your heart and do not lean on your own understanding; In all your ways acknowledge him and he will make your paths straight."*

I recall how I felt on the evening of November 4, 2012. I was amazed to learn that Barack Obama had been elected to a second term as president. The following thoughts and emotions came flooding upon me: Isn't this the guy who just a few short weeks ago was resoundingly defeated in arguably the most one sided presidential debate in history? After all this guy has done, and not done, in the past four years, and the American electorate still wants him to be president? I sadly and erroneously came to the same conclusion that millions of other Americans came to... it's over. The misinformed, the uninformed, and the takers have finally outnumbered the well informed, the engaged, and the productive.

This queasy feeling engulfed me for weeks until I looked at what had happened from a different perspective. If all or a healthy number of thoughtful citizens had turned out at the polls, and this was what they came up with, then my initial assessment of what had transpired would have been correct. But that is hardly what happened. Once I emerged from the fog of discouragement, I did a little research.

According to the Providence Forum, only 50% of Evangelical Christians in America are registered to vote. Of that number, only half generally show up. This figure was fairly accurate in the 2012 presidential election. Furthermore, there were countless other conservative-minded citizens who would not consider themselves Evangelicals, who stayed home that election night as well.[29]

Although Evangelicals make up a fairly large voting bloc, the reality is that there are a lot of Evangelical Christians who simply don't vote. The number of U.S. citizens who are of voting age and are eligible to vote—a major distinction, as there is an aggressive push to encourage illegal aliens and felons to participate in this sacred process—is roughly 62%. This figure ebbs and flows, given the importance of the election (national vs. off-year). However, I would contend that we should never look at *any* election as an off-year election. Although a pathetic figure, I'm not going to go off on an "everyone should vote" rant. If you don't know the names of your representatives, what your state capital is, and cannot name the three branches of government, I'd rather you stay home. However, if you have thoughtfully researched the issues, I will drive you to the polls myself even if your views are different from mine.

If we as believers truly believe that God should be involved in every decision we make, we should be very troubled that only about half of the Christians in America are registered to vote. Their reasons for not registering are pretty similar to those given by many citizens: "they're all a bunch of liars anyway; my one vote is not going to make any difference; it really doesn't matter who gets elected; they're not going to change this messed up system; etc." You would hope that Christians, who at least profess to care about faith-based issues, would be less cynical, but they're not.

Even more disturbing is the fact that of those faith-based citizens who are registered to vote, only 50% actually make it to the polls. If you are concerned enough to register you would think you could go all the way and actually vote but apparently it's not that simple. When the smoke clears, we are left with the sobering reality that 75% of Christians in this country don't vote. Mind boggling, but true. Edmund Burke said it best: "The only thing necessary for the triumph of evil is for good men to do nothing." In 2010, a few more good men and women took it upon themselves to do something. In that election, the number of faith-based voters who showed up at the polls spiked from the usual 25% to 30%. Numerous local, state and federal executive and legislative branches were transformed. These newly elected, principled public servants are forwarding faith-based agendas and oftentimes thwarting legislation that believers would find destructive to our nation.

The 2010 midterm elections were a classic example of grass-roots efforts to elect individuals who would effect change, not just take up space. Conservatives in this country have finally learned from their political opponents on the left that change, in any form, is always more profound and long-lasting if it comes from the ground up rather than from the top down. Top-down change is good, but it often comes from political pressure rather than any true change of heart from those involved in making or executing policy. Don't get me wrong, I'll take change for the good, even if my elected representative is kicking and screaming throughout the process. However, political pressure usually doesn't happen without numbers. Movements, regardless of merit, are much more effective with numbers. When everyday, ordinary citizens wake up to what is going on in this country and then actually work to do something about it, the country will change for the better.

One would hope that a born-again believer would be a little more inclined to take an interest in who governs or legislates in this country but this is not the case. One of the reasons might be that both Evangelicals and non-Evangelicals view politics in a negative light. The American Heritage dictionary defines politics as "The art or science of government or governing, especially the governing of a political entity, such as a nation, and the administration and control of its internal and external affairs." Do you see anything in that definition about lying, cheating, or stealing? I don't either.

People who are corrupt give politics a bad name, and we should be ashamed of ourselves for repeatedly voting for corrupt individuals. People who advocate "changing the system" often miss the point. Our system of government (a representative republic) is the greatest system the world has ever seen. The system doesn't necessarily need to be changed as much as the system needs to be purged of corruption. As we learn from the definition, politics is a necessary thing in our society. If Jesus took an interest in politics, then so should we.

One of the many reasons the Pharisees wanted to kill Jesus is because he exposed them for the political frauds that they were. The Pharisees were every bit as much of a political entity as they were a religious group. Like it or not, when you stand up in any forum and start espousing absolutes like Jesus did, you've entered into the political discussion. Was Jesus a politician? Absolutely not! However, to say that Jesus wasn't concerned with the issues of the day is ludicrous. So we have to get over the fact that politics in this country (and more so in other countries) is an ugly business.

We've all seen voter guides that are designed to "inform" the public or, more specifically, a particular voting bloc, on where the candidates stand on particular issues that happen to affect them directly. As stated already, churches are well within their legal rights to disseminate these voter guides (even from the church premises). But I'll do you one better: We all have access to the greatest voter guide ever written: The Holy Bible! *Any* issue we need to research before we make an informed voting decision can be found in the Bible.

But be careful: Many "believers" have written books, articles, and blog entries about what God thinks about the issues we face. The trouble with some of these "believers" is that they pluck verses out of the Bible, (completely out of context) to fit God's opinion into *their* political agendas. Scripture should be checked against Scripture and should always be viewed in the context within which it was written. God is not a Republican or a Democrat. When informing ourselves about the issues, we must always find out what God thinks about it and then proceed from there.

Accessing a candidate's voting or governing records is easy. Visit the candidate's website and search for their voting record. If their website doesn't include that information, there's something wrong. If they have such a good voting record, why would they hide it? Why do *you* have to hunt for it? Unfortunately, citizenship is a fulltime job. If someone's rhetoric is consistent with their record, they should have no problem chronicling that record.

The voting records of all current legislators in any political body can be found by going to the website of that particular body. Additionally, there are several Christian voting organizations, like Eagle Forum, Heritage Alliance, and Providence Forum, which provide voter guides that reference the ultimate voting guide, the Bible. In addition to voting records, some of these organizations ask questions of the candidates. If a candidate declines to answer a simple, forthright question from a bona fide Christian voting organization, that's a big red flag. Not wanting to go on record about an important issue probably means that the candidate is personally not too concerned with that issue, or feels that a clear, unequivocal answer may cost votes. In God's eyes, this is an example of the tail wagging the dog.

So after going down your list of issues that you feel are important to God, which in turn means that they are important to you, your family, and your community, how should you proceed? Is there a specific criterion we must follow when selecting a candidate? Let's say on five key issues that you feel are important to God, both candidates are great on the top two but no so great on the others. What do we do? What if they are both great on all five? What if they're both abysmal on all five? Do I pass on voting at all?

Most of the time, if you've done your homework, your choice is clear. When it gets a little more confusing, ask God for help. James 1:5 says *"If any of you lacks wisdom, you should ask God, who gives generously to all without finding fault, and it will be given to you."* Personally, I believe God is more concerned with an issue like abortion than He is about something like oppressive taxation, even though the latter will indeed hurt the family. So with this in mind, one might opt for a candidate who is pro-life yet consistently votes for higher taxes such as Senator Robert Casey (D) from Pennsylvania, over a pro-choice candidate who consistently votes for lower taxes such as Scott Brown (R) from Massachusetts. This scenario is unlikely, but possible, and thoughtful Christian voters have to use their brains *and* their Bibles, should choices like this present themselves.

Other choices are not as difficult, as most candidates legislate or govern in a manner that is generally either pleasing or offensive to God. It's those scenarios where the candidate's records are a little quirky or inconsistent where extra thought is required. If, however, a candidate is clearly woeful on the top issues as God sees them and you still want to vote for them, you'd better start looking in the mirror. Putting your party affiliation or a candidate's charisma before your willingness to obey God is precisely how ungodly candidates get elected.

In the spirit of getting along, should we expect our politicians to compromise with their political opponents? Before we go any further, let's look at the definitions of a few words that we need to understand before we answer this question. Compromise: "The settlement of difference in which each side makes concessions." Concession: "The act of conceding." Concede: "To acknowledge, often reluctantly, as being *true, just or proper*, admit. To yield or grant a privilege or right." As previously stated, if you define the verbiage, then you win the war.

In today's lexicon, compromise is a good thing. One who compromises is often thought of as amiable, accommodating, and generally a nice person. However, many politicians in positions of great power and influence have simply lost their way. Sadly, some have never had any semblance of good judgment, yet they are in positions of great power. Do you think Jesus wants our elected representatives to "compromise" with individuals like this, or legislatively "defeat" these individuals? The answer to me is quite clear.

How our elected representatives express their differences is certainly something Jesus is concerned with, but whether these representatives should stridently oppose their political opponents, who legislate in a manner that is indifferent or hostile to the concerns of faith-based voters, should not be up for debate. In the legislature, we often hear rhetoric from some that suggests that there is too much partisan bickering in politics. If only these candidates would reach across the aisle in a conciliatory fashion to their political opponents, they might actually get things done.

When I hear rhetoric like this, I cringe. Bad policy is bad policy, and politicians forwarding such policy should never be comprised with. In an attempt to appear to be working on your behalf, many politicians will get along, reach across the aisle, or essentially compromise on issues that are vitally important to the survival of this nation. Many of the laws that this country was built upon were directly crafted with the Ten Commandments in mind. Should our lawmakers compromise on these principles just because some in our land don't subscribe to them? Certainly not, but God help us if they do!

IS THERE EVER A REASON NOT TO VOTE?

Let me first start by saying that, in general, it's a good idea to vote. In order to reshape America, it is incumbent upon God-fearing, country-loving, and *informed* individuals to vote. However, in my opinion, there are circumstances in which it is okay not to vote. Let me strongly state that this option should never be taken lightly and never be steeped in emotion. Furthermore, simply staying home is never an option. What I mean is that your decision to not vote should never be a blanket declaration to never vote again or to simply skip an election cycle. The times I have not voted were in specific races; I have never stayed at home on Election Day.

The times when I have not voted fall into two categories. The first is rare (depending upon where you live), but it is when both candidates are so odorous that I could not physically pull the lever for either one. This is a scenario where both of the candidates aren't too concerned with faith-based voters. Not only does their record stink, but they're not even going through the motions to sound like they might represent you or your family in a decent manner. The second scenario is a little deeper and requires some explanation. We've all heard of voting for the lesser of two evils. That's when one candidate is bad but the other one is worse.

We are often encouraged and sometimes even intimidated into voting for the lesser of two evils by friends, family, co-workers, and party apparatchiks. Many thoughtful voters, particularly faith-based voters, have fallen prey to the following guilt trip: If *you* don't vote for X, then you're helping Y to get elected! Last I checked, it was incumbent upon the *politician* to earn my vote, rather than having to hold my nose and chuck my and, more appropriately, God's criteria out the window.

The natural consequence of this phenomenon is that candidate X will ultimately surf down as close to candidate Y as they can without offending you "too much." They are banking on the fact that we "Jesus freaks" would never vote for candidate Y as long as candidate X is "a little better" than candidate Y on those pesky social issues. Although that line between candidates X and Y seems to get blurrier every year, candidate X gets our vote, especially if their rhetoric is replete with words like *God, church, family,* etc. These candidates are sometimes taught a lesson, as the voting bloc that they usually bank on stays home altogether, and they are defeated. Thankfully, faith based voters are starting to become a little more wary of candidates who play the "Jesus card." Donald Trump is someone who attempted to play that card at a speech to Evangelical Christians at a Values Voters Summit. Someone should have told Mr. Trump that faith-based voters are generally not stupid people. They may be far more gullible than they should be but they are not stupid. It was quite apparent to me that Mr. Trump was using the Bible as a prop. He appeared stiff and unnatural even holding it, let alone referring to it. This is dangerous territory to wade into and I think it illustrates how grossly naive Mr. Trump is when he speaks to religious people. His former and current positions on many faith-based issues are at variance with the word of God. His rhetoric toward anyone who disagrees with him is hardly Christlike. If you're going to hold the Bible when speaking to a group, at least look comfortable doing it. Allude to its contents once in a while, discuss how its tenets shape your life at every turn, don't use it as a tool to curry favor with a particular voting bloc.

Candidate X has more to worry about than trying to fool faith-based voters. Despite the fact that candidate X may govern or legislate in a manner closer to the word of God, they are in dangerous territory as Galatians 6:7-8 tells us *"Do not be deceived: God cannot be mocked. A man reaps what he sows. Whoever sows to please their flesh, from the flesh will reap destruction; whoever sows to please the Spirit, from the Spirit will reap eternal life."* As reprehensible as many of candidate Y's policies may be, at least they have the decency not to play the "Jesus card" like candidate X often does in order to pander for votes. Remember, candidate X, every knee will bow before the Lord.

Finally, there is no perfect candidate. If you are withholding your vote until a candidate comes along who governs or legislates and conducts themselves in a manner that is in lockstep with God, you'll simply never vote. Do your homework and seek God's wisdom in prayer, and you will vote for the correct candidate.

So how do we proceed after we've gone to the word of God and educated ourselves on what God has to say about the issues? The next step is to analyze the legislative or governing record of the individuals who want our vote. We must do this because what they say is often wildly inconsistent with their actions. This disparity between what politicians do and say is even more breathtaking, given the fact that their voting or governing history is 100% verifiable! Many politicians are betting on the fact that most won't even attempt to verify that their deeds are inconsistent with their rhetoric.

Sadly, experience has told them that this is a very safe bet. A large percentage of voters do not do any research on a candidate's record. This phenomenon has spawned the term "low information voter": A person who cares enough to vote but is unwilling to put the necessary time and effort into researching potential candidates. They glean bits and pieces of information through dubious social media sources, sensational sound bites, and, believe it or not, comedians. It takes a little effort to do the research properly.

A bona fide source of information can be up to anyone's interpretation, depending upon your political bent. However, to a Christian, the bona fides of the Bible are never in question. *If* one desires God's guidance on how to vote, political affiliations and personal preferences are rendered meaningless. Ephesians 5:17 says, "*Therefore do not be foolish, but understand what the Lord's will is.*"

ACTION STEPS

1. Ask yourself: What am I doing to affect positive change in the area of politics?

2. Research the personal and legislative records of our leaders. Do they square with the word of God?

3. Ask the Lord if He would like you to do more in this area.

4

Social Justice

Social justice means many different things to many different people. Glenn Beck, a prominent radio and television personality, author, public speaker, and CEO of Mercury enterprises, defines it as "the forced redistribution of wealth, with hostility to individual property, under the guise of charity and/or justice." He further adds, "I doubt many churches in America would agree with that."[30]

Franklin Graham, son of the incomparable Billy Graham, is a world-renowned pastor in his own right, an author, and the President and CEO of the Billy Graham Evangelistic Association and Samaritan's Purse, one of the largest humanitarian gospel organizations in the world. His view on social justice differs wildly from that of many liberal Christians. Although he and his ministry wholeheartedly support the notion of helping the poor, sick, disadvantaged and marginalized, he insists on not doing it at the expense of the gospel.

In an interview with *The Gathering* a few years back, Reverend Graham asserted that if the social program comes *first*, and then, if you can, you try to work the gospel wedge into it, it won't work. It has to be the gospel first. He goes on to say, "And by the way, if I see someone hungry, I'm going to try to feed them. If I see someone who needs medicine, I'll give him that...But I'm going because Christ told me to go into the world and make disciples. He never told me to go feed people. He never told me to go try and make people feel better. He told me to preach the gospel."[31] If we are not careful, we can really misinterpret Reverend Graham's words.

His point of putting the gospel first is a good one to remember when discussing the ever growing social justice movement. I'm with the social justice folks in their quest to be more Christlike in terms of helping disaffected individuals. However, if their primary focus is on "helping" the individual, they are missing it. If our primary focus is not on the gospel, we will slowly but surely spend so much time helping those who are socially marginalized that we will start to overlook and, worse yet, make excuses for many of the reasons that they are marginalized. Many of these disaffected individuals, who we should indeed help, are steeped in sin. To simply downplay or not even address this misses what God is all about. Social justice activists contend that God is about love; this is true, but He is also about right and wrong as well.

Dr. Tony Campolo, pastor, author, and accomplished speaker, says social justice is nothing more than love transformed into social policy. Sounds wonderful, but the devil is in the details. To Mr. Campolo's credit, he goes on to say, "Christians do agree that they should love, and they agree with social justice being transformed into social policy but they don't always agree on how to make that transformation."[32] I'll say.

Jim Wallis is a renowned author, public speaker, pastor, and founder of Sojourners, a progressive Christian organization whose mission is to articulate the biblical call to social justice, inspiring hope and building a movement to transform individuals, communities, the church, and the world. Sounds benign enough, but to answer the biblical "call" without focusing first on what the Bible has to say about several of today's pressing social issues is disingenuous. It is far easier to dupe and manipulate the masses if your definition of social justice is superficial and platitudinous.

Wordsmithing is essential to this movement if you desire to curry favor with the lay person or, sadly, the uninformed and apathetic believer. As I have stated countless times, you define the verbiage, you win the war. Although I will address illegal immigration in detail later, now would be a good time to illustrate how the use of words can quite effectively take one's focus off the real issue. People on the left in general, and in the social justice movement in particular, have effectively taken the focus off of the illegality of entering or residing in this country without doing what is necessary to become a citizen. They have sufficiently shamed more than a few Americans to stop calling illegal aliens what they are: illegal aliens.

Calling us out for not being as sensitive as they, we were urged to call them "illegal immigrants." When illegal immigrant was too judgmental, we were compelled to use the phrase "unauthorized immigrants" which was soon replaced by "undocumented immigrants." The press and the Obama Administration have again redefined this class of individuals as "Americans in waiting." The laws on illegal immigration are clear and unambiguous. Can they and will they change? Of course, but until there are wholesale changes in immigration law, they are what they are.

If the individuals who don't subscribe to the notion that they should obey these laws continue to flout them, we are at an impasse. We are primarily at this impasse because of a dearth of principled politicians who insist that we should enforce the laws. Until we get principled politicians, or the laws on immigration change, this issue will continue to smolder. Social justice activists understand very well that the best way to effect a change in policy is to change the verbiage. A softening in rhetoric may be sold as "Christlike," yet its unintended or, more often, intended consequence is to shame people into loving the lawbreaker, while distracting them from the lawbreaking itself.

I'm all about loving the sinner, but an inordinate amount of time, energy, and resources on loving the sinner to the exclusion of any appreciable amount of hatred for the sin renders God's word irrelevant. Warren W. Wiersbe said, "Truth without love is brutality and love without truth is hypocrisy."[33] God's word is incredibly comprehensive. The natural result of picking and choosing the parts you like is a troubling phenomenon called the "inclusive church." If these churches were inclusive in the biblical sense of the word, I would be all for them. But their "inclusion" is often code speak for, "Come as you are, we're not gonna judge you today, tomorrow, and most likely never."

Spending all our time and energy on all the presumed social injustices out there leaves little time to actually "minister" to those poor sinful souls in the areas in which they need it most. Social justice activists presume to be more loving than those on the Christian right (and a lot of times they are). However, how loving is it to never address the 800 pound gorilla in the room: SIN? To allow anyone to languish in sinful behavior while asserting that you are a "loving" Christian is delusional and sad.

Many in the social justice movement feel that government should do more to help the poor and downtrodden in this country. They take to heart Paul's word in Romans 13:1: *"Let everyone be subject to the governing authorities, for there is no authority except that which God has established. The authorities that exist have been established by God."* Although I agree wholeheartedly with Paul's words, we must look at the historical record of all governments as we assess their role in any facet of our lives.

Governments, even relatively sound, stable governments, have had a history of governing in unthinkably godless ways. Blindly accepting the premise that government can do better for the poor than citizens and the civic and religious organizations they belong to is simply not true. The incredibly noble motives that civic and religious organizations have in helping the poor—to exhibit the love of Christ and lead people into a saving relationship with Him—are always preferable to the myriad of ulterior motives government has in "helping" the poor.

Speaking of ulterior motives, did you hear what presidential candidate Hillary Clinton stated in a *New York Times* interview? She said, "At the risk of appearing predictable, the Bible was and remains the biggest influence on my thinking. I was raised reading it, memorizing passages from it and **being guided by it.** I still find it a source of wisdom, comfort and encouragement."[34] I believe Mrs. Clinton when she says she is comforted and encouraged by the Bible. However, if you deem something to be a source of wisdom, one would think you would heed the wise advice contained within that source. Mrs. Clinton's personal conduct and legislative record are often in direct conflict with the word of God. Mrs. Clinton would do well to read James 1:22-24 which states: *"Do not merely listen to the word, and so deceive yourselves. Do what it says. Anyone who listens to the word and does not do what it says is like a man who looks at his face in a mirror and after looking at himself, goes away and immediately forgets what he looks like."*

Let's talk about envy. Envy is "a feeling of discontent and resentment aroused by and in conjunction with desire for the possessions or qualities of another."[35] Envy is the one of the biggest problems we have in this country. There are many reasons why envy is such a destructive force, the biggest being that it takes our focus off of God and puts it on something else.

There are countless biblical passages about envy. James 3:16 says, "*For where you have envy and selfish ambition, there you find disorder and every evil practice.*" Proverbs 14:30: "*A heart at peace gives life to the body, but envy rots the bones.*" 1 John 4:8: "*Whoever does not love does not know God, because God is love.*" We are literally ripping the fabric of this country apart by our preoccupation with what other people have, how they got it, and what they do with it. Many Americans are guilty of this without even realizing it. Some Christian leaders also use envy in an ignorant attempt to put God in a box as it pertains to "social justice." Still other Christian leaders, and politicians in particular, know full well what envy does, and they perpetuate it anyway. This is wrong.

Although 1 John 4:8 does not mention envy or jealousy directly, it does get to the heart of the problem: a lack of love for one's fellow man. Why don't some of us love our fellow man? Because he's got more stuff than we do! He's richer, his kids get As in school, he has a beautiful big house and he drives a luxury car. For some, that's enough to hate someone. For these folks, and their numbers are growing, the antidote to this problem is not any introspective analysis of why *they* don't love their fellow man, but a much more base remedy to this problem…take the rich guy's stuff! Now some do this quite literally in the form of theft, but many others subscribe to a less radical, yet no less troubling, alternative: oppressive taxation.

I'd like to say this in nicer terms, but we need to call it what it is. The war on the rich in this country has never been this strident. Sure we have always had one class or another resenting someone from another class. We've even had governments, tyrants, dictators, or kings, etc. exploiting this phenomenon in order to manipulate the masses. However, a more recent and troubling twist to this exploitation has been the call by none other than Pope Francis himself for more wealth redistribution from the "haves" to the "have nots." In his address to the United Nations, Pope Francis said, "An awareness of everyone's human dignity should encourage everyone to share with complete freedom the goods which God's providence has placed in our hands."[36]

If Pope Francis stopped there, I'd be okay with his comments. However, he wades into dangerous territory when he lectures us on *who* should be facilitating said sharing. He tells us that a contribution to equitable development could be made "both by international activity aimed at the integral human development of the entire world's people and by *legitimate redistribution* of economic benefits by the *State.*" The UN has a long and storied history of looking the other way on a whole host of atrocities carried out by many of its member states. Not only have they turned a blind eye to the economic raping and pillaging of the downtrodden by dictatorial and tyrannical regimes, but they themselves, as a collaborative body, have been up to their eyeballs in fraud and mismanagement of funds earmarked to help the poor and oppressed. Are we so naïve to think that the UN or any of its corrupt member states will exercise the "legitimate" redistribution of funds to the world's unfortunate?

Perhaps Pope Francis should look to the writings of one of his predecessors, Pope Leo XIII, for some guidance. Leo XIII, commenting on socialists working on behalf of the poor by exploiting their envy of the rich, said the following:

> *Socialists by endeavoring to transfer possessions of individuals to the community at large, strike at the interest of every wage earner, since they would deprive him of the liberty of disposing*

of his wages, and thereby of all hope and possibility of increasing resources and of bettering his life condition.[37]

To put it plainly, Robin Hood economics fosters anger and resentment rather than love and compassion. This is exponentially true when the entities that are engineering the transfer have absolutely no concern for the poor themselves. By depriving an individual of voluntarily disposing of his goods or wages, the state foments anger and resentment among the "haves" of the world. Let us refer to Paul's comments in 2 Corinthians 9:7: "Each man should give what he has decided in his heart to give, not reluctantly or under compulsion, for God loves a cheerful giver." Being urged by God to give of the goods that God's providence has placed in our hands is a far cry from being forced to give of these goods by an often godless state whose motives having nothing to do with the word of God. However, today we have an emerging and very troubling phenomenon.

Bible believing folks, often very well meaning, are being whipped up by "leaders" in the church who are forwarding a concept of social justice. I put the term leaders in quotes because true leaders inspire and lead by example. The opposite of this is someone who divides and is hypocritical. Sadly, we have a lot folks in politics and in the religious community who divide and conduct themselves disingenuously. To illustrate this, let's review Matthew 6:1-4:

Be careful not to practice your righteousness in front of others, to be seen by them. If you do, you will have no reward from your Father in heaven. So when you give to the needy, do not announce it with trumpets, as the hypocrites do in the synagogues and on the streets, to be honored by men. I tell you the truth, they have received their reward in full. But when you give to the needy, do not let your left hand know what your right hand is doing. So that your giving may be in secret. Then your Father who sees what is done in secret, will reward you.

Don't get me wrong, there are folks within the social justice movement who are generous with their own money and are genuinely concerned for the poor. However there are some who are very much like the religious leaders in Jesus's day, who feign concern for the poor in order to make themselves look righteous. Jesus had contempt for exploitation of the poor, and He has it today as well. Social justice advocates in the religious community work in tandem with politicians in order to "help" the poor by demanding that more money be spent to remedy a wide array of social injustices; however, it never ceases to amaze me how generous politicians can be with other people's money. At least the Pharisees did indeed give to the poor, albeit in a very public way.

Today's politicians have been routinely embarrassed when their public rhetoric on giving does not jibe with their own checkbooks. Furthermore, the poor are not political pawns to be used to attain or retain political office. I realize that public policy concerning funding for the poor is indeed public, but there are plenty of times that we can help the poor privately. I believe Jesus had this in mind in Matthew 6:1-4. Not only do Jesus's words warn us about giving for the sake of appearing righteous, but I believe Jesus is also concerned with the dignity of the poor. When giving is discreet and non-public, the poor have been aided and not humiliated. Although being poor is nothing to be ashamed of, we are indeed human beings with feelings. To respect those feelings indicates a *true* heart for the poor rather than *using* the poor as props for ulterior motives.

When it comes to social justice, politicians tend to have very short memories when it comes to inconsistencies between what they say and what they do. In a *Washington Post* interview, Hillary

Clinton's friend and former speechwriter, Lissa Muscatine said, "Methodism is a really huge source of *personal* spirituality to [Mrs. Clinton]—she's very religious, which most people don't know about her." The first question I would ask Mrs. Clinton's friend is, "Why don't we know this about her? Other than the disingenuous and hackneyed response, "my religion is very private to me," there's another reason.[38]

The real reason in the minds of many Americans (particularly faith-based voters) is Mrs. Clinton's behavior and legislative record aren't remotely Christlike. There are numerous examples of this, but I think her comments at the 2015 Women in the World Summit is illustrative of her priorities as they pertain to God and the law, or in *her* world, The Law and God, in that order. She asserts that, "Far too many women are still denied critical access to reproductive healthcare and safe childbirth. All the laws we've passed don't count for much if they're not enforced...[D]eep-seated cultural codes, religious beliefs and structural biases have to be changed."[39] Obviously "reproductive healthcare" and "safe childbirth" are codespeak for abortion. Mrs. Clinton continually fails to realize that you can't have your cake and eat it too. Invoking God in the form of touting your Methodist roots to curry favor with faith-based voters and then publicly declaring that the God who influences her life must look the other way on abortion is outrageous and illogical. As with many people who use Jesus to further their careers, they will ultimately answer to Him for their actions.

However, Mrs. Clinton may not be so unpopular with some Christians, particularly those who fancy themselves as "progressives" whose ideologies on social justice differ dramatically from traditional Evangelical Christians. Ms. Muscatine goes on to state that Mrs. Clinton's religion is the driving force for her commitment to social justice, that it led her to start initiatives that fought against human trafficking, promoted maternal health care in developing countries and, above all, inspired her to fight for women's rights. As noble as these endeavors may or may not be, they cannot blur her record on the rights of unborn children. Or can they? Organizations whose sole purpose is to blur the lines between right and wrong are popping up at an alarming rate. One such group that has been around for a while, but is sadly more relevant in today's whacked-out world, is the Religious Coalition for Reproductive Choice (RCRC). Groups like this make it infinitively easier for politicians like Hilary Clinton to appear consistent when she touts her belief in God and then legislates in a godless manner.[40] According to their website, the RCRC asserts that personal decisions such as terminating a pregnancy are best left up to a woman to discern for herself, in consultation with her family, her *faith*, and others she might bring into the conversation. I would humbly suggest that they bring *God* into the conversation! You see, "faith" is basically anything you want it to be. You can have faith in *a* god rather than faith in *the* God. The one true God would never condone abortion. The RCRC homepage goes on to state that "There is no religious consensus on when life begins" I guess Jeremiah 1:5, *"Before I formed you in the womb I knew you, before you were born I set you apart,"* doesn't resonate with some "religious" people. There may not be a religious consensus but there most certainly is a consensus on this issue among people who believe the Bible. Finally, the RCRC's declarative statement on their website pretty much illustrates the ideologies of the more radical wing of the social justice movement. It reads: *We have stood arm in arm with proponents of comprehensive sexuality education, worked for a version of the Affordable Care Act* (ObamaCare) *that included contraception with co-pays, and we were instrumental in bringing faithful* (not necessarily godly) *voices of those at the pulpit, in pews and in communities across the country to issues such as the Violence Against*

Women Act, the approval of Plan B pills and telemedicine for abortions and for the ability of servicewomen to access abortion care while serving our country. We believe in faith expressed in action. Yes you do and people who think like you are growing at an alarming rate. It is incumbent upon thoughtful, Bible-believing Christians to reach out in love to these individuals by pointing them to Gods word. If we don't, they will continue to run interference for politicians like Hilary Clinton and countless others who attempt to use their faith in God as a tool to garner votes.

The danger of the social justice movement within the Christian community is that its devotees often selectively champion noble and sometimes not so noble social causes with laser beam focus, yet they are seemingly unconcerned by other social ills. Many reference John 8:7: when Jesus says to the teachers of the law and the Pharisees, *"Let any one of you who is without sin be the first to throw a stone at her."* They reference this verse to illustrate a legitimate social ill: judging. However, you almost never hear the same individuals highlighting Jesus's words a few verses later in John 8:11 when he commands the adulterous women to *"Go now and leave your life of sin."* No one likes to be judged, so by focusing on the sin of judging, they've championed a cause that resonates with everyone.

However, by ignoring or simply giving lip service to the sin of adultery, the Christian left again illustrates the selective outrage in which they often engage. Jesus never diminished the magnitude of the woman's lawbreaking as He extended His love and compassion. He illustrates perfectly in these verses what is meant by the phrase "Love the sinner but hate the sin." I don't understand why this concept is so hard to understand. We love our kids but hate their bad conduct, don't we? Social justice Christians do a very good job of loving as it pertains to "loving the sinner," but their hatred of sin leaves something to be desired. Sadly, their hatred of those who hate the sin is a lot greater than their hatred of the sin itself. A failure to thoughtfully reconcile the concept of loving the sinner but hating the sin inevitably leads to anarchy.

Some sins are deemed no biggie and others are to be stamped out with a vociferous movement. These selective causes seem not to be determined by the scriptures as much as they are by the political winds; this is troubling. Taking scripture out of context or presuming we know how Jesus would want us to deal with social issues without any scriptural reference is frightening. As it pertains to selecting a candidate to vote for, this "selective" vetting process can lead to disastrous results. Such an example can be found in the Clinton supporters that have organized a "Faith Voters for Hillary" website, which highlights how she would serve religious communities as president.

The apostle Paul has some sound advice for any Christian who may be wooed by a candidate whose words and deeds might not jibe when he warns Christians in Romans 16:17-20: "*I urge you, brothers and sisters, to watch out for those who cause divisions and put obstacles in your way that are contrary to the teaching you have learned. Keep away from them. For such people are not serving our Lord Christ, but their own appetites. By smooth talk and flattery they deceive the minds of naïve people.*" Christians have the ultimate guidebook in the Holy Bible and should never be put into the category of "naïve people." If we are exploited, it is often our own doing.

SAME-SEX MARRIAGE

The Supreme Court of the United States, in a 5-4 ruling, found that the Constitution does indeed guarantee the right to same sex-marriage. In his dissent, Judge Clarence Thomas invoked the Declaration of Independence, stating, "Our Constitution—like the Declaration before it—was predicated on a simple truth: One's liberty, not to mention one's dignity, was something to be shielded from—not provided by—the State. Today's decision casts that truth aside...The government cannot bestow dignity, and it cannot take it away."[41] Chief Justice John Roberts, in his dissent, said, "The majority's decision is an act of will, not legal judgment. The right it announces has no basis in the Constitution or this court's precedent. The majority expressly disclaims judicial 'caution' and omits even a pretense of humility, openly relying on its desire to remake society according to its own 'new insight' into the 'nature of injustice.' He went on to say that the court's accumulation of power does not occur in a vacuum. It comes at the expense of the people.[42] Perhaps the most scathing of the dissenters' comments came from the honorable Justice Antonin Scalia who, like his fellow dissenters, refuses to even comment on the rightness or wrongness of same sex-marriage (unlike the majority of his colleagues who took every opportunity to do this) but instead focused on his role and the role of the esteemed body that he belongs to. Judge Scalia said, "So it is not of special importance to me what the law says about marriage. It is of overwhelming importance, however, *who* it is that rules me. Today's decree says that my Ruler, and the Ruler of 320 million Americans coast to coast, is a majority of the nine lawyers on the Supreme Court." He further states, "The opinion in these cases is the furthest extension in fact—and the furthest extension one can even imagine—of the Courts claimed power to create 'liberties' that the Constitution and its Amendments neglect to mention. This practice of constitutional revision by an unelected committee of nine, always accompanied (as it is today) by extravagant praise of liberty, robs the People of the most important liberty they asserted in the Declaration of Independence and won in the Revolution of 1776: the freedom to govern themselves."[43]

By now, some of you may have checked out with all this "judicial stuff." Let me try to bring you back. The reason I've cited these judges is that our friends in the social justice movement have clearly displayed a pattern for disregarding what God has to say about numerous issues. They have opted to focus almost entirely on injustices (as perceived by the state) as far more important than injustices perpetrated against God's laws. With this in mind, it behooves one to get acquainted with how same sex-marriage came to be sanctioned, as whether God sanctions it or not seems to be a matter of indifference to many in the social justice movement. I would assume these individuals would have a big problem with Rowen County Clerk Kim Davis who was thrown in jail for refusing to issue marriage licenses to same-sex couples. This tortured logic starts when society values the opinion of five robed social engineers more than the principles of God who breathed the universe into its very existence. It's profoundly sad that the average American doesn't understand that Mrs. Davis's first amendment right to freely exercise her religion (without fear of being locked up) trumps any constitutional contortions in which the Supreme Court cares to engage. Don't get me wrong: if the opportunity to thoughtfully and respectfully debate the issue of where the Bible stands on homosexuality presents itself, go for it. However, if the person you are trying to reason with simply chooses to ignore what Scripture says about same-sex marriage then you're not going to persuade them (at least not in one meeting). It may be preferable in the short term, to argue the unconstitutional nature of the decision itself in order for them to understand what happened on 6/26/15. As much as the decision was offensive (and should be) to many Christians, the bigger picture was the unconstitutionality of the decision. The reason we should understand and subsequently focus on what is occurring in the Supreme Court is that more and more of this nonsense will occur concerning many moral issues that are of great concern to God. To put it simply, we are now in an era where all three branches of government are legislating. It is sadly ironic that the Executive and Judicial branches are actually more strident and purposeful in their legislative actions than the Legislative branch itself. All of this is happening while most Americans sit back and watch this dysfunctional circus, if they're paying any attention at all. Bringing everyone back to the Bible as it relates to every hot political issue is still what we are charged to do. However, at the same time we must also remind our fellow citizens that our system of government comprises three co-equal branches of government that are charged to do very different things. Our president is making laws and declaring things to be just because he'd like them to be. And as we see on a regular basis, our Supreme Court routinely drags causes across the finish line with no regard to the merits of the law that may or may not support these causes. The five justices who let their preference for same-sex marriage trump their judicial responsibilities are very similar to our friends in the social justice movement. Both individuals are refusing to submit to those they serve. In the case of the Supreme Court, it is We The People. In the case of the Christian in the social justice movement, it is God. Both individuals are out of bounds and need to be told so.

But who is going to talk sense into the Christian who thinks the church should calm down about same-sex marriage? Well it won't be the Presbyterian Church. As is the case with a growing number of denominations, this issue is ripping apart congregations all across America. A woman named Marie had the misfortunate (or maybe it was God's calling) of finding herself in the thick of intense debates on this issue at each of the last two churches she attended. After watching her Episcopal congregation fracture on this issue, she found herself in the same situation at the Presbyterian church she now attends. Her pastor, who quickly realized that Marie was a very thoughtful, Bible-believing congregant, recruited her to step out of her comfort zone and voice her concerns over the church's rapidly evolving views on same-sex marriage.

Marie was a ruling Elder on a board that was charged by the local church's governing body, Presbyterian Church USA, to vote on whether or not same-sex marriages could be held on church premises. Presbyterian Church USA took the easy way out by not taking a clear stand, instead leaving it up to local pastors to decide if they would officiate at same-sex marriage ceremonies. Although many pastors refused to perform such ceremonies, that didn't settle the issue as many pastors who choose not to perform these ceremonies allow them to be conducted at *their* church by others. So much for the pastor being the leader of the church. These boards were instructed by Presbyterian Church USA to "vote your conscience" and not necessarily what's best for the congregants. Do you think "consult the Holy Spirit living inside you" might have been a little more helpful advice?

While many thoughtful congregants stood around flat-footed, many other congregants' consciences were being worked on by gay couples who had recently joined the church. Their "God doesn't want us to judge" and "remember, we need to be welcoming" mantras unfortunately swayed enough board members to vote for allowing the church to perform same-sex marriages on their local church's premises. The vote wasn't even close.

We should always be welcoming. Jesus wants us to come to Him just as we are but eventually, sooner or later, we must acknowledge why we come to church in the first place. It's not to be entertained in a comfortable environment; it's to become educated about God's principles. Sometimes this educational process can be uncomfortable, but it's still necessary. The function of the church should be to lead people to Jesus Christ and, once saved, educate them on how to be more like the person who saved them, period. The rest is far less important. Many in the social justice movement expend such an inordinate amount of time and energy on everything but education that the greatest educational resource ever written, the Bible, becomes a prop rather than the living, breathing Word of God. This disproportionate concern with people's feelings manifested itself, as it often does, in the board members not even citing Scripture as they felt it would be too "judgmental" since the only one who even bothered to cite Scripture to put a stop to this was Marie, the outcome was inevitable. Even her pastor, a voting member of the board, wasn't too forceful in the process as he didn't want to be perceived as a bully. Soft-spoken Marie was left to fight this fight the only way she knew how: with Scripture. Even though her side lost, she gained so much more in the long run in terms of pleasing her creator. Regardless of the outcome of the vote, you know He will say, "Well done, my good and faithful servant" when they meet.

Ephesians 5:31 says that *"For this reason a man will leave his father and mother and be united to his wife, and the two will become one flesh."* Although the Bible is pretty clear on this issue, there are actually more than a few folks on the Christian left who are willing to look the other way. These folks have a problem with those on the Christian right who vehemently quote Scripture that roundly condemns homosexuality and then take it up a notch by vehemently condemning gay people without spending a whole lot of time trying to love them. This is a fair criticism. John 13:34-35 says, *"A new command I give you: Love one another. As I have loved you, so you must love one another. By this everyone will know that you are my disciples, if you love one another."*

Conversely, our friends on the Christian left obfuscate wildly by asking questions like: "Why is the Christian right obsessing about this when there are so many other social problems that the church should be concerned with?" It's actually quite easy to tackle *all* issues regarding moral conduct and social decay without conveniently picking and choosing the ones that fit a particular agenda. Further complicating things, you have a growing number of Christians who believe that the condemnation of homosexual behavior is actually a social injustice in and of itself. Take the case of Carla Hale, a former physical education teacher at Bishop Watterson *Catholic* High School. Further complicating things, you have a growing number of Christians who believe that the condemnation of homosexual behavior is actually a social injustice in and of itself.

Battles seem to be erupting routinely pitting churches against employees who feel that they are being discriminated against because they are gay. Before I opine on this phenomenon, let me state unequivocally the following; If someone who is currently employed or is seeking employment in the public sector, is being unjustly discriminated against because of their sexual proclivity, not only do I sympathize with them about this wrong but I think they should take to the streets to protest this clear violation of the law. However this scenario is not even remotely related to the aforementioned conflicts churches are having with current and prospective gay employees. I think the issue is summed up rather clearly and succinctly by the following statement that was released by the Catholic Church in reference to their stance on this issue. "The Catholic Church respects the fundamental dignity of all persons but also must insist that those, whom it employs, respect the tenants of the church."[44]

As reasonable as this statement may be to some, it's anything but reasonable to a growing number of others. These individuals on the Christian left feel that their "social" Catholic teachings actually call them to act when they see an injustice such as not allowing openly gay individuals to remain employed or seek employment with the church. Is the injustice that is being perpetrated against Gods word equally disturbing to those same individuals? Unfortunately for many it is not. Selective moral outrage is a very dangerous thing and is the cornerstone of the social justice movement.

A growing number of churches have attempted to blur the lines when it comes to homosexuality by marketing themselves as "welcoming" to homosexuals. Make no mistake about it, *all* denominations should be welcoming to homosexuals. Those that do not will have to answer to God for their lack of compassion. This includes churches that feign being a welcoming church but, as evidenced by their behavior toward homosexuals, are anything but welcoming.

These churches that market themselves as welcoming go out of their way to display rainbow logos in order to court gay parishioners. Such churches seem to be very much concerned with the unloving and indifferent treatment other churches display toward homosexuals (and they should be). But are these "welcoming" churches far less concerned with the act of homosexuality itself? The Bible is a very comprehensive book. Jesus expects us to have enough room in our heart to be loving, caring, and welcoming and still point wayward people in the right direction.

On the subject of homosexuality, loving and teaching are not mutually exclusive concepts. In fact, Christ can't do what He would like to do in the life of the homosexual if the church practices one of these without the other. Even more troubling are the churches (and I do use this term very loosely) such as the Westboro Baptists, who are neither loving nor very good at effectively teaching when it comes to homosexuality.

Unfortunately, to more than a few, they are the face of Christianity. In an odd way, the more Westboro Baptist-type Christians there are, the more some churches feel the need to be "welcoming" or, should I say, "Welcoming to the exclusion of any judgment whatsoever as it pertains to conduct that is offensive to God." Pope Francis's recent visit to the United States left both social justice-types and Christians who are concerned with such beliefs sort of scratching their heads. While in Philadelphia, the Pope told the hundreds of thousands who came to see him that "Our common house can no longer tolerate sterile divisions."[45] At first blush this seems to be a rather innocuous statement steeped in common sense. But the mere fact that the quote means different things to different people illustrates the Pope's hesitance to boldly and specifically call certain types of sinful behavior wrong. To many in the social justice movement, the statement is a breath of fresh air to an often acrid discussion about sin and the sinner's responsibility for that sin. The problem lies with one's personal interpretation of "sterile divisions." Many in the social justice movement are so hypersensitive to even the mild admonishment of sinful behavior that they could take this statement to mean a moratorium on any judgment levied by fellow believers. To that I would argue, what's the point of being a church if not to point people to Jesus Christ and His principles? I would like to think that Pope Francis's comment was geared more for those of us in the body of Christ who seem to be incapable or unwilling to unite rather than divide, to attract rather than repel.

Pope Francis gave some indication of what he meant later in his address with a thought-provoking question for his followers: "I leave you with a question, a question for each of you to answer: In my own home, do we shout, or do we speak to each other in love and tenderness? That's a good way of measuring our love." As much as his final comments were spot-on, some wished he would have been more forceful and clear when he addressed Congress a few days earlier. Critics cited the fact that he never said the word "abortion" but instead opted to remind us of our responsibility to protect human life at every stage of development. Critics went on to note that the phrase "same-sex marriage" was never uttered as the Pope opted for a gentler approach, saying that fundamental relationships are being called into question. To be fair, the Pope was a bit more forceful and specific when addressing his followers in New York and Philadelphia; however, little excuse can be offered for the fact that the name of Jesus Christ was not invoked even once in his address to Congress. Lecturing our representatives on "environmental stewardship" and the "ills of political polarization" seems a bit odd when Rome is literally burning. We have a big problem in the body of Christ when the causes and agendas of Christians become more important than Christ himself. During times as perilous as these, the name of Jesus Christ should have been uttered by Pope Francis regardless of his fear of being politically incorrect.

ACTION STEPS

1. Research numerous credible sources and find out what social justice is all about. Be forewarned, the term means different things to different people.

2. Find out if the principles and causes of individuals in this movement are scriptural in nature.

3. Find out where your church stands on issues of social justice.

4. Find out what your church is doing to address social injustices in our society.

5. Ask the Lord to soften your heart to those in our society who are victims of true social injustice.

5

Do We Value Life?

Jeremiah 1: 4-5 says: "*The word of the Lord came to me saying, 'Before I formed you in the womb I knew you, before you were born I set you apart; I appointed you a prophet to the nations.*" To me, this one's pretty clear: God hates abortion. Many Christians feel that when injustice becomes law, resistance becomes duty. Now, you may be one who isn't comfortable protesting at abortion clinics, and I respect that. At the least, we can resist by voting for pro-life candidates. Some pro-choice politicians have had genuine epiphanies, come to their senses, and become pro-life. Others, strangely enough, have had epiphanies in the opposite direction and became pro-choice. Dick Gephardt, Dick Durbin, Bill Clinton, and Al Gore are a few who have experienced a change of heart and became pro-choice after being pro-life.

The Gore flip-flop is especially troubling, given that he was once devout enough to major in divinity at Vanderbilt University's prestigious divinity school for three semesters. Still retaining something of a moral compass, Gore voted pro-life 84% of the time as member of the US House of Representatives. Sadly, his position on abortion turned on a dime once he became a US Senator. Still others have had *several* changes of heart on the issue; Mitt Romney is an example. From declarative statements such as, "I believe that abortion should be safe and legal in this country" to "I am firmly pro-life"[46] with numerous tortured variances of both positions in between, Governor Romney is certainly conflicted on this issue. Or is he?

A one-time change in thought could generously be described as an epiphany; several changes of thought are, no doubt, political expediency. Many politicians of different parties are pro-abortion. They are not pro-choice as they would contend, they are pro-abortion. Condoning some abortion is just as bad as condoning a lot of abortion, or even advocating for the practice.

Amazingly, when it comes to abortion, we have lost the ability to *think*. According to a recent Gallup poll, 58% of Americans oppose all or most abortions. As a pregnancy progresses and the baby becomes larger, a fair amount of the population (including most who identify as pro-choice) start to get a little queasy with the issue as only 10% of Americans think that partial-birth abortion should be legal.[47] Notice I didn't use the term "late-term abortion." Our society will continue to lose its ability to rationally discern right from wrong if we allow ourselves to be influenced by people who are determined to put lipstick on a pig and tell you that it's not a pig.

Dr. Kermit Gosnell is one of those people who tried to put lipstick on a pig. For years in his abortion mill in West Philadelphia he routinely performed what he called late-term abortions. Unfortunately, at least ten, and most likely a lot more, of his procedures went terribly awry. Dr. Gosnell was not fazed by the fact that these babies, who survived his attempts to kill them, started to move and cry and actually *act* like babies. He would tell his nurses and technicians that the babies were not living or moving but simply showing reflex responses.[48] I am not going to share the jokes he told about these babies or the ghoulish manner in which he finished what he set out to do, but let's just say that he will have to answer to God for what he has done.

Planned Parenthood is one of many groups to exploit the tragic rash of shootings of young black men in this country. Regardless of your opinions on how and why Travon Martin, Michael Brown, and Eric Garner were killed, the fact remains that black lives do matter. Again, selective outrage seems to be the order of the day for our friends on the left. The last group on the planet (including the Ku Klux Klan) that should feign concern for the black community is Planned Parenthood. If you find the last sentence flippant and distasteful, please consider this: Abortionists kill more black babies in a week than the KKK has in the past 100 years![49]

The temerity of Planned Parenthood to insert themselves into a movement which asserts that black lives matter is reprehensible. To put this into perspective, ponder the fact that abortion has claimed the lives of sixteen million black people in the last forty years. African Americans account for 13% of the population in the United States, yet they account for a staggering 40% of all abortions. If these individuals had been allowed to live, *African Americans would make up 36% of the US population.* Although *all* God's children are precious in His sight, I would like to implore pastors who lead predominately African American churches to prayerfully consider these sobering statistics when deciding which politicians they are allowing into their scared pulpits. Unfortunately, most who lock in on churches such as these to stump for votes are pro-abortion. Thoughtful pastors of predominately African American churches are starting to say, "Enough is enough!" They have no doubt been swayed to re-think who they invite to their churches by the latest news reports/videos capturing Planned Parenthood executives cavalierly discussing the sale of baby parts with would-be buyers. But for the rest of these pastors who seem to have no reservation whatsoever in inviting people who support this group into their pulpits, I'd like you to consider the following quotes from Planned Parenthood's founder Margaret Sanger:[50]

"We don't want the word to go out that we want to exterminate the Negro population." Mrs. Sanger, a renowned eugenicist, knew it was necessary to conceal her ideologies from the general public when embarking on her mission to provide "Reproductive Health Care" to the women of America. She knew that she needed to be shrewd when dealing with potentially distrustful African American women who were somewhat apprehensive about the concept of birth control. Mrs. Sanger stated that: "We should hire three or four colored ministers, preferably with social service backgrounds, and with engaging personalities. The most successful educational approach to the Negro is through a religious appeal." If the ultimate goal of the extermination of black people started to become apparent to these women, Mrs. Sanger states that "the minister is the man who can straighten out that idea if it ever occurs to their more rebellious members." Some things never change as many black pastors either look the other way or are unbelievably supportive of the racist organization that Mrs. Sanger founded.

"They are human weeds, 'reckless breeders,' 'spawning... human beings who never should have been born." These thoughts were targeted toward immigrants, the poor, and what she termed "the error of philanthropy," Her contention was that *"Birth control is nothing more than...weeding out the unfit."* Birth control was an effective way of preventing the birth of defectives or those who will become defective. Or, in her words,

"Human beings who never should have been born at all." All of these chilling quotes by Planned Parenthood founder Margaret Sanger can best be summed up by Dr. Alveda King, civil rights activist and niece of Dr. Martin Luther King, Jr., who said, "The most obvious practitioner of racism in the United States today is Planned Parenthood, an organization founded by the eugenicist Margaret Sanger and recently documented as ready to accept money to eliminate black babies."

Thankfully there are not a lot of Kermit Gosnells out there, but there are plenty of seemingly sane individuals who, in one form or another, look the other way when it comes to abortion. When the young mother views an ultrasound image of her twenty-week-old baby sucking her thumb, she correctly surmises that there is, indeed, a living child inside her womb. Is this baby of more value as it is grows inside mom's tummy? Apparently it is to some, as evidenced by the percentage increase in Americans who are okay with the abortion of a zero-to-six-month-old fetus but have some serious concerns with a fetus being aborted that is six-to-nine-months old. This illogical disconnect can only be the result of hard-heartedness. Hebrews 3:12-13 says, "*See to it, brothers and sisters that none of you has a sinful, unbelieving heart that turns away from the living God. But encourage one another daily, as long as it is called today, so that none of you may be **hardened** by sin's deceitfulness.*" The charade of calling a baby a blob of unviable tissue was easier to perpetrate before the advent of technology. You would never dream of valuing your three-year-old son over your one-year-old son because he's smaller, would you? Thankfully, not everyone in this great land of ours has lost their ability to think and feel.

North Dakota Governor Jack Dalrymple recently signed legislation banning abortion if a fetal heartbeat can be detected; this can happen as early as six weeks into a pregnancy.[51] Babies that are six weeks in-utero are not out of danger however. In order to detect a heartbeat at this early stage of life, a woman would have to undergo a vaginal ultrasound. Pro-abortion advocates have successfully pressured states not to require moms to have this diagnostic procedure, arguing that it is "too invasive." The tortured logic involved in claiming that a vaginal ultrasound is too invasive to the mother, but a partial-birth portion is not too invasive to the child is incomprehensible. North Dakota is also the first state to sign into law legislation banning abortions based on genetic defects. This ban sends a clear message to pro-abortion advocates that the state of North Dakota values *all* life, as does our Lord in Heaven.

As much as some battles in the abortion debate are influenced by the massaging of the English language, some battles are not. The Born-Alive Infants Protection Act (BAIPA) is one such example. I vacillated a bit on taking too much time chronicling President Obama's governing and legislative history on the abortion issue. However, failure to do so would be to ignore the elephant in the room. I opted to at least spotlight his views when he was in the Illinois legislature representing the Thirteenth District.

Jill Stanek was a Christian nurse who worked in the labor and delivery department at Christ Hospital in Oak Lawn, Illinois. When Jill found out that babies who survived abortions were being left to die without proper medical intervention, she knew that she could not keep silent. When she spoke up, she was told by her administrators that the practice would continue and in 2001 she was terminated for her refusal to remain quiet. Her written testimony has been front and center in debates on this issue in the Illinois State House and the US Congress.

As you might imagine, reading pages and pages of legislation, and the interpretation of such legislation, would require several hours of one's time and effort, so let me attempt to synthesize this material so you can have at least a working understanding of then-Senator Obama's views on this issue. Given that the BAIPA addresses procedural protocols *after* a child is born, one has to wonder who Barack Obama was pandering to when he cast the votes he did. His strident, unwavering support of something many would consider infanticide is chilling under normal circumstances, but such conduct from someone who professes to have "Jesus in my heart" is unfathomable.

Alan Keyes, who opposed Obama in his bid for the United States Senate, said it best: "Christ would not stand idly by while an infant in that situation died." In a nutshell, BAIPA legislation defines any aborted fetus who shows signs of life as a "born-alive infant," which entitles them to legal protection, even if doctors believe it could not survive. The last part of the statement is critical as pro-choice individuals have the audacity to assign greater value to human beings who happen to be lucky enough to have made it to a chronological age that *they* deem worthy of respect.

Obama opposed the bill in 2001 and 2002, as he viewed it as a backdoor attack on a woman's legal right to abortion. He goes on to say that he would have been in full support of a similar bill that President Bush signed into law in 2002, as it contained protections to uphold the integrity of Roe vs. Wade. In an attempt to pass this critical legislation, the Illinois bill was amended in 2003 to include such a clause.

The language in the Illinois house bill was now nearly identical to the bill President Bush had signed into law. This clause stated: "Nothing in this section shall be construed to affirm, deny, expand or contract any legal status or legal right applicable to any species of the homo-sapien at any point prior to being born alive as defined in this section." Despite including this provision, the revised bill, SB1082, never made it to the floor of the Illinois House, as it was blocked by the Health and Human Services Committee chairman, Barack Obama.[52] As previously stated, Barack Obama is simply doing what millions of Christians do on a daily basis: he is taking his Christian hat on and off depending on the situation.

Unbelievably, President Obama made the following statement in a USA Today interview: "Aborting babies alive and letting them die violates no universal principle." Huh? Who does he think blinked the Universe into existence? Who are we to assign a hierarchy of worth to the principles that the creator of the Universe laid out? President Obama later thought it would be wise to soften his comment, but his revision is no less troubling:

> *"If I am opposed to abortion for religious reasons but seek to pass a law banning the practice, I cannot simply point to the teachings of my church. I have to explain why abortion violates some principle that is accessible to people of all faiths, including no faith at all. If a man is not governed by his principles either godly or ungodly, how good of a leader can he be?"* [53]

Explaining tough decisions or placating various constituency groups is not leading, it's following. Abortion is wrong in the eyes of God and the President's *first* allegiance should be to Him. John 14:15 says *"If you love me, keep my commands."*

Unfortunately, for every victory there are just as many defeats. Judge Edward Korman ruled that the Plan B morning-after pill must be made available over the counter to women of *all* ages! Yes, that includes girls aged sixteen and under.[54] As if your job as a parent wasn't difficult enough! Personally, I would not vote for a pro-abortion candidate. Many, particularly in the Northeast, don't have the luxury of choosing between pro-life and pro-choice candidates, as they all are typically pro-choice.

However, there is hope. Recently, media exposure of unspeakable practices has resulted in public outrage in the treatment of the unborn. Kudos to the media in the United Kingdom for exposing the horrific practice of using aborted babies for energy. Addenbrooke Hospital burned 797 aborted babies in their "waste to energy" furnace which heats the facility. How shameful not only to refer to God's precious creations as "waste," but to add insult to death by abusing these babies further, treating them as one would a piece of coal or a stick of wood. Thankfully, once the light of day was shown on this unspeakable practice, the UK Department of Health banned the practice.[55]

Sadly, we don't have to look abroad for such barbaric behavior as such practices go on right here at home. There is a high probability that human fetal remains contained in medical waste were used to generate electricity at a Marion County, Oregon waste-to-energy plant. Again, because of investigative efforts by religious groups, and subsequently, the media, the practice of incinerating aborted fetuses as an energy source will be far less likely in the future. Local officials acted swiftly to enact legislation that requires infectious medical-waste haulers to provide certified documentation stating that their shipments do not contain human fetal tissue.[56] Such instances may seem like small victories, but every flood is started by a couple raindrops.

EUTHANASIA

You may have an awareness of where your representatives stand on issues like abortion, gay marriage, taxes, etc. How about euthanasia? That doesn't seem like a hot topic on the political scene. Well, maybe not today, but one has only to look to the Netherlands to see what is coming down the pike. Once you understand what has happened over there in the last twelve years, you should have reason to be concerned, especially as our baby boomer generation enters middle and old age.

Euthanasia is the act or practice of ending the life of an individual suffering from a terminal illness or incurable condition as by lethal injection or the suspension of extraordinary medical treatment. If the subject of euthanasia isn't worrisome enough, throw "physician-assisted suicide" into the mix, and then we Americans have real cause for alarm. Individuals have been ending their own lives for centuries. Although there are laws on the books citing this as illegal, states have more or less looked the other way when it came to an individual deciding to end his own life. Recently, states have gone beyond looking the other way and have started passing laws sanctioning this practice by doctors who are regulated by, and are under the authority of, the states.

Euthanasia has been legal in Belgium, Luxembourg, and the Netherlands for a number of years. Here in the United States, as of 2016, Washington and Oregon allow physicians to legally assist patients in ending their lives. So much for the Hippocratic Oath! However, proponents of physician-assisted suicide contend that the physician is not doing any harm; in fact, they are helping patients die with dignity. Rita Marker, an authority on the public and private aspects of euthanasia, said it best when she said, "Social engineering is always preceded by verbal engineering."[57] By calling doctor-assisted suicide "death with dignity," you have cunningly crafted the verbiage and thereby have successfully marketed a concept as something that it isn't.

Barbara Wagner of Springfield, Oregon, asserts that she is not ready to die, stating emphatically, "I've got things I'd still like to do!" Barbara has cancer, yet she was heartened as her doctor offered some hope by informing her of a new chemotherapeutic drug called Tarceva. However, the Oregon Health Plan sent her a letter saying that her cancer treatment was not approved. To be fair, this does happen all across the country, and insurance companies do have the right to deny coverage for drugs or procedures they deem to be "new" or "experimental." However, the State of Oregon added insult to injury by stating in the denial letter that they *would* pay for comfort care, including "physician aid in dying," better known as assisted suicide. Barbara was incredulous, telling them, "Who do you guys think you are? You'll pay for my dying but you won't pay to help me live longer?"

Oregon physician Dr. William Toffler asserts that the state has a financial incentive to offer death instead of life. Chemotherapy drugs cost $4,000 a month, while drugs for assisted suicide cost less than $100. The irony is that while Oregon is denying Mrs. Wagner legitimate pharmaceutical agents for her cancer it has recently determined that diabetes is now a terminal illness, making a diabetic eligible for a lethal prescription.[58] This is frightening stuff!

Although I will talk about the Patient Protection and Affordable Care Act in greater detail in Chapter 8, I'd like to comment on section 1233 of the bill now, as it pertains to the topic of euthanasia. As you may recall, when President Obama started to sell the idea for ObamaCare, he made the now infamous comment "your Grandmother may opt for a pill rather than a procedure." By oversimplifying the complexity of end-of-life medical choices, the president clearly illustrated why we need less bureaucratic involvement in our healthcare system rather than a massive infusion of it as will be the case under ObamaCare. Penny Young Nance, president of Concerned Women for America, summed it up well when she said that "Unelected and unaccountable bureaucrats will decide what treatments our elderly patients receive. No longer will we be able to make decisions in conjunction with medical professionals about our parents' needs; these decisions will be decided by reimbursement rates set by an inauspicious board." By "unaccountable," Ms. Nance means that ObamaCare quite plainly exempts these boards from *any* legislative, judicial, or executive branch oversight. Chilling stuff, if you ask me.

Although proponents of these boards assert they are necessary to control rising health care costs, the unintended or *intended* consequence of such boards will undoubtedly be the rationing of healthcare. The rationale of proponents of these Independent Payment Advisory Boards (IPABs) is that there is an exploding need for health care and only limited funds to even attempt to fulfill this need. Someone has to reign in these costs. At first blush, this sounds mildly logical. However, by anyone's estimation, certain categories of Americans are simply going to be denied or severely restricted as it pertains to what type of health care they will receive as they age.[59]

A panel of unelected and unaccountable bureaucrats when posed with the question "Does Grandma *need* that artificial hip?" will simply refer to some sort of actuarial table or chart to determine that she only has a few years of unproductive (as determined by the state) years left, as opposed to a fellow American who has several *productive* years left that needs the same type of prosthetic. Prosthetic devices cost a lot of money, and when rationing—always a byproduct of socialized medicine—is the determining factor in the treatment of patients, grandma is going to be out of luck. I hope that pill that President Obama was referring to is effective, as grandma's degenerative condition will be very painful. So where does euthanasia come in? Well if an IPAB can deny your grandmother an artificial hip to cut down on Medicare costs, think what could be saved by their suggesting that your grandmother simply fade off into that good night. After all, she had a good life. Why burden the health care system with all those inevitable end-of-life medical costs? Who cares that Psalm 71:9 says, "*Do not cast me away when I'm old; do not forsake me when my strength is gone.*" The proponents of these Draconian measures assert that the Bible and its principles are antiquated and our desire to help grandma simply needs to change with the times.

Even though the Netherlands is at the forefront of making this practice very easy, they do have some checks and balances in place. Two doctors must agree that there is no chance of recovery, and the patient must be fully conscious when requesting to be euthanized. Furthermore, the physicians must agree that the patient is experiencing "unbearable and interminable suffering." Not content with those weak, yet somewhat logical, criteria, a growing number of citizens in the Netherlands are determined to take this to the next level.

Enter what some call "euthanasia on wheels": mobile units that travel around the country, assisting patients whose own doctors refuse to help them die because they are concerned with the patient's ability to perform euthanasia, or they feel that assisting in the procedure would violate their moral or religious beliefs. Not to worry, these mobile teams are equipped with a doctor, a nurse, and all the medical equipment necessary to carry out euthanasia.

The bottom line is that when God is missing from the equation, things like this happen. If you have no God in the equation, no thoughtful and competent physician in the equation, no rational government agency that respects the tenets and laws of our creator, what are we left with? The tail wagging the dog.

Don't get me wrong; I am a huge proponent of patient's rights. I feel patients should be well educated on their disorder in order to assist their physician with a treatment plan. However, there's a reason that God is God; there's a reason that doctors must successfully complete twelve years of higher education; there's a reason that our legislators should have a better understanding of the issues. The reason that God and these individuals are put in place is to protect us from policies such as doctor-assisted suicide. When we as a society choose to leave God out of the equation, we will be hopelessly at the mercy of godless, heartless, and agenda-driven individuals who exploit our ignorance and naïveté.

ACTION STEPS

1. Research the Bible to find how much God values life.

2. Ask yourself: How much time do I really spend thinking about the lives of the unborn, infirmed, and elderly?

3. Ask yourself: What am I doing to save, improve, and impact the lives of this nation's most vulnerable?

4. Ask God to reveal to you what He'd like you to do on behalf of these people.

6

Illegal Immigration

Every country has things in its history that it isn't proud of, and every country is currently engaging in activities that are detestable to God. Having said that, the United States, with all its warts, has been and will always be the most tolerant and welcoming nation on Earth. Despite this, more than a few in this country don't feel this way. They focus on our faults while overlooking the fact that the majority of us *want* individuals to immigrate to our great land, but only as long as their motive for coming here is to make the country a better place. We welcome with open arms people who would produce rather than take, to love this country rather than hate her, and ultimately, to assimilate rather than Balkanize.

It's estimated that there are roughly 11.5 million illegal aliens currently in the United States.[60] Whether you use the term illegal immigrant, illegal alien, or undocumented immigrant, the fact remains that they are in this country illegally. It's helpful to under-stand why they are here, but their reasons for being here rarely justify how they came to *be* here. Many progressive Christians who advocate for "social justice" will go to extraordinary lengths to pervert Scripture in an attempt to minimize the problem of illegal immigration, often citing Exodus 22:21: *"Do not mistreat or oppress a foreigner, for you were foreigners in Egypt."*

Perhaps our friends on the left would prefer other translations which refer to these folks as sojourners or strangers. I am not averse to using these terms. However, regardless of the term we use, what they have done to get into this country is wrong. As we've previously discussed, a clever trick employed by the Christian left is to pay lip service to the sins of man, while adroitly moving to the love of Christ while demonizing folks on the Christian right who don't exhibit that love. To that ploy, I say, "two out of three ain't bad." Do we need to work a whole lot harder to exhibit the love of Christ toward illegal aliens? Absolutely. Do we have to call attention to Neanderthals on the Christian right who "don't like them thar foreigners?" Absolutely. However, focusing on those two points and merely glossing over the original sin is a recipe for anarchy.

The main reason the majority of illegal aliens come to this country is to make money. The bulk of them come from Mexico which suffers from a poor economy. However, just because one wants to increase his chances at prosperity, he cannot use illegal means to do it. In *Greed and Oppression of the Poor*, by K. Scott Schaffer, the author asks, "Does God give us the right to keep the needy away from our prosperity?" A loaded question to say the least. To be fair to Mr. Schaeffer, he does comment on how issues of national security and crime should be taken into consideration when making laws pertaining to illegal immigration. However, the verbiage used in the question itself is carefully selected in order to divert our focus away from the law breaker and on to evil capitalism.[61]

Back to Exodus 22:21: do we mistreat the illegal alien when we deport or penalize him? The fact that a sin has been committed by these folks is, to me, obvious. What to do about the sin is much more complicated. Disrespecting any nation's sovereignty by having no regard for their rules of lawful inhabitance cannot be tolerated. Otherwise, what's the point of having a sovereign nation? Civilized, God-fearing nations have standards and ideals by which they choose to live. Entering a country lawfully and with a desire to not only assimilate but to make that nation better is something we as Americans should encourage.

So, where should the politician I vote for stand on illegal immigration? I believe a politician's stance should be the following: first, secure our border. This is only logical triage. Leviticus 24:22 says, *"You are to have the same law for the foreigner and the native born. I am the Lord your God."* You don't spend an inordinate amount of time fixing an injured man's broken leg when he has no pulse. The amount of time and money it would require to secure our border is infinitesimal compared to the massive amounts of taxpayer money we waste on frivolous endeavors every day. The common sense, first step solution to border security (building and reinforcing a secure fence on our nation's borders) is sadly and unbelievably ripe for demagoguery. When advocates for open and unfettered borders incredulously assert that American citizens want to "build a fence" to curtail this problem, it is an attempt to demonize the vast majority of us who thankfully don't see reasonable border security as unloving.

Are we proposing to construct a Berlin-type wall here? Have we so lost our minds that wanting to have a technologically sound and secure fence around our nation is tantamount to mistreating aliens? What's next? Will these un-Christlike, "documented" xenophobes dare to suggest security systems at business establishments, armed law enforcement, even locks on our front doors? You get the point.

If the United States can put a man on the moon almost half a century ago, we can build a technologically secure fence on our nation's border in a few months. A handful of Amish men can raise a house in a day, for goodness' sake! Building such a fence would be cause for concern if we were ruled by any other form of government, but we have a long history of being welcoming to a fault and securing our borders is a good idea supported by the vast majority of Americans.[62] I would be very suspect of any politician who spends an inordinate amount of time talking about amnesty with nary a mention of border security. On the other hand, I would be equally wary of any politician who spends all of their time talking about border security, without forwarding some compassionate, thoughtful ideas that could lead illegal aliens on a pathway to citizenship.

John 8 recounts:

The teachers of the law and the Pharisees brought in a woman caught in adultery. They made her stand before the group and said to Jesus, "Teacher, this woman was caught in the act of adultery. In the Law Moses commanded us to stone such women. Now what do you say?" They were using this question as a trap, in order to have a basis for accusing him.

But Jesus bent down and started to write on the ground with his finger. When they kept on questioning him, he straight-ened up and said to them, "Let any one of you who is without sin be the first to throw a stone at her." Again he stooped down and wrote on the ground.

At this, those who heard began to go away one at a time, the older ones first, until only Jesus was left, with the woman still standing there. Jesus straightened up and asked her, "Woman, where are they? Has no one condemned you?"

"No one, sir," she said.

"Then neither do I condemn you," Jesus declared. "Go now and leave your life of sin."

Jesus's response should not lead us to assume that He was not concerned with the law and the consequences of breaking it. His response is not a refutation of the law but a call to all of us to treat lawbreakers (sinners) with compassion and forgiveness. Again, plucking verses out of the Bible to buttress arguments is dangerous. To focus on Jesus's compassion by quoting the first part of John 8:3-11 without addressing His final words to "Go now and leave your life of sin" is willfully ignoring the issue of sin.

Sometimes when we sin, Jesus disciplines us in the midst of forgiving us. The consequence for the sinful act of entering this country *illegally* can't be cavalierly dismissed or the *"Go now and leave your life of sin"* part of the verse has no meaning. If a reasonable punishment or penalty is not levied on those individuals who are currently in our country illegally, they and millions of other future illegal aliens will get the message loud and clear that America simply does not care about the rule of law.

The aforementioned right-wing Neanderthals are just as guilty as many progressive Christians when it comes to picking and choosing Scripture. Focusing on Jesus's final words to the woman, which address sin, while blowing by verses 3-10, which refer to forgiveness, is equally troubling. Someone who is presumably on the Christian right should not be so obsessed with a monolithic, homogenous society where everyone looks and acts the same. They should not care how many *legal* immigrants this country welcomes annually as long as they appreciate the Judeo-Christian principles this country was founded on and are willing to assimilate into the culture with the intention of making America a better place. We are called a melting pot for a reason.

If you look at the early church, and many great Bible-believing churches today, they are made up of a wide array of congregants from very different economic, social, and racial strata. Progressive Christians need to do more than accurately quote their unloving, hyperjudgmental right-wing Christian cousins when urging us to minimize the illegal immigrant issue. Making these individuals the face of the anti-illegal alien movement is a disingenuous, yet effective, way to demagogue this issue. Add some perversion and omission of instructive Scripture and it's easy to see why Christians are torn. The church will continue to be divided on this and several other issues if Christians refuse to put agendas aside and study the word of God *in its entirety* when seeking God's thoughts.

Finally, President Obama doesn't help things. He seems to be growing impatient with Congress's inability to effectively deal with the illegal immigration problem, so he has done something about it. The timing of his action is curious, but I would rather focus on his invocation of Scripture to help sell his plan to unilaterally create an amnesty, or a path to American citizenship, for five million illegal aliens. It wasn't the first time, and it certainly won't be the last, that a politician has implied or outright said that God is on their side on a particular issue. I am certainly not averse to this, as the premise of my whole book is based on the acronym WWJD (What Would Jesus Do?); however, if your reason for quoting Scripture is to push your political agenda across the finish line by implying that God's down with your policies, then be prepared to have *all* your policies scrutinized by folks who actually take the Scriptures seriously.

You can't pick and choose Scripture to use, or more appropriately misuse, while simply ignoring other Scripture altogether. An ironic example of this is the rhetorical question Obama posed to the American people in his amnesty speech. He asked us if we were a country that's about ripping children out of the arms of their mothers. Being concerned about children who are ripped out of their mothers' arms while indifferent to the plight of children who are ripped out of their mother's wombs is the height of hypocrisy.

And, Mr. President, please don't *knowingly* take Scripture out of context to further your agenda, whether the agenda is God-inspired or not. President Obama seemed to be quoting Exodus 23:9—"*Do not oppress a foreigner; you yourselves know how it feels to be foreigners, because you were foreigners in Egypt.*"—but his actual words were "Scripture tells us that we shall not oppress a stranger, for we know the heart of a stranger, we were strangers once too. We are and always will be a nation of immigrants... We were strangers once, too." The aliens, foreigners, sojourners, or strangers (depending upon what translation you are reading from) that the Bible refers to in Exodus 23:9 were Israelites who were forced into slavery by Egyptian oppressors. The strangers to whom President Obama would like to grant amnesty have certainly come to this country of their own volition and are hardly oppressed slaves. Regardless of this convenient and inaccurate characterization of the modern-day illegal alien, God still wants us to treat them fairly and compassionately. What "fairly" means could easily take an entire book to attempt to explain; however, the difficult job of tackling the illegal immigration issue is made infinitely harder when demagogues on both the left and the right knowingly distort and pervert Scripture.

Finally, US District Court Judge Andrew Hanen has issued a ruling that has at least temporarily blocked President Obama's landmark immigration overhaul. The case was before the judge as a result of a lawsuit filed by 26 states who asserted that the Obama Administration exceeded its power by deferring the deportation up to five million illegal aliens. Judge Hanen said "The court finds that the government's failure to secure the border has exacerbated illegal immigration into this country," and "The record supports the finding that this lack of enforcement, combined with the country's high rate of illegal immigration significantly drains the state's resources." However, his ruling that the Obama Administration failed to comply with the Administrative Procedures Act was the ultimate reason for the Department of Homeland Security putting new immigration programs on hold.

The Administrative Procedures Act requires that any proposed rules or regulations must appear in the Federal Register in order to give the public a chance to digest and comment on proposed policy. This act was put into place so presidents couldn't turn into Kings enacting policy by executive fiat. *Prior* to his executive order, President Obama is ironically on record (22 times) making statements such as: "For me to simply through executive order ignore those congressional mandates would not conform with my appropriate role as president," "I am President, I am not King. I can't do these things by myself," and "I can't just suspend deportations through executive order, that's just not that case."

These pronouncements have left the administration dancing on the head of a pin. In an attempt to downplay the monumental nature of his edict to suspend deportations, President Obama made the assertion that his actions are no different than previous Republican presidents. The glaring difference between his executive order and the executive orders of past administrations is that past presidents have augmented immigration policy which had *already been approved by Congress* rather than making a presidential edict as a result of *Congressional inaction* on immigration reform.[63]

ACTION STEPS

1. Research numerous, credible sources to get a general view of what the illegal immigration issue is all about.

2. Study the Bible to see what God says about illegal immigration.

3. Find out what your political leaders are doing about illegal immigration.

4. Ask the Lord for wisdom before you enter into a discussion with fellow citizens about illegal immigration.

7

Economics

Bob and Suzy have limited funds. He is a manager at a manufacturing plant who earns $52,000 a year. Suzy is a stay-at-home mom, raising two children. She also waits on tables for six hours every Saturday morning. Her hourly wage plus tips yields her $125 for her efforts. They have lived in the same modest home for the last seven years and would like to start looking for a bigger home for their growing family. They do not lead an extravagant lifestyle. They have very limited savings ($5,000 for emergencies) which they try not to touch. They're a pretty typical American family.

A financial dilemma has arisen in their household. After a pretty rough winter, they notice that there is a tiny drip coming from their living room ceiling. They were clued into the problem by a foul odor which began wafting from the living room. Sure enough, their very expensive carpeting was starting to stink as dirty water slowly dripped onto it from a leak in the roof. The most palatable of several estimates put the cost of the repair at $7,000! Bob, frustrated and reactive, declared that they would have to just "put a bandage on" the problem for the foreseeable future.

You see, Bob is "handy," (I try to tell my wife that there are *some* advantages to having ten thumbs) and his wheels are already turning, figuring out how to fix this problem. Suzy, on the other hand, has been down this road before and has a good memory. She knows all too well that cheap is always expensive in the long run. Although Bob's the "fix-it" guy, Suzy is the *homemaker* (a term often pilloried, but in this case appropriate), and her perspective is going to be very valuable in this instance. She recalls quite vividly the things she saw, smelled, and felt when looking for their first home years ago. She knows that if their roof is not *properly* fixed the re-sale value of their home could plummet.

As we said, Bob and Suzy are going to start looking for a bigger home. This bigger home will cost more money, so the more money they can demand for their current investment the more they can defray the cost of their next one. A discolored ceiling and the smell of a wet carpet will not help them sell their house for top dollar. Additionally, if this problem is not fixed promptly, they will have to replace a perfectly good carpet with another expensive one. While never usurping her husband's leadership role in the home, Suzy asserts her right to bring her valuable perspective to the discussion. After joint prayer, Bob realizes the incredible value of Suzy's opinion and his reluctance to break the piggy bank for the repair slowly abates. He even suggests that they take out a very small loan so they are not left with nothing in their savings should another emergency be around the corner. This is an example of *good* debt. The short-term debt that the family has incurred is money well spent in comparison to a diminished resale value of their home.

Jim and Patty are Bob and Suzy's neighbors. They live paycheck to paycheck and really don't have any savings to speak of. Jim has been promised a raise at work, but he has heard this from his boss for a long time, and no such raise has materialized. Patty owns a large SUV that she and her three small children drive around in. It gets poor gas mileage, but it's safe and reliable. Jim, on the other hand, drives a much smaller vehicle, which he complains about from time to time. After five years, Jim has just cleared his final car payment and would like to upgrade to something a little bigger.

His current vehicle has 85,000 miles on it but still runs well. He is well aware that other such makes and models routinely run for 200,000 miles. Despite this, Jim is bent on getting a new car. Patty doesn't think they should bite off another loan so soon after they just finished paying off the last one. Jim feels slighted at work and has convinced himself that at this stage of his life he deserves a nicer, roomier car. After no prayer and a few pseudo-discussions with Patty, Jim unilaterally pulls the trigger on a new car. This is an example of *bad* debt.

Now I'm no Milton Friedman, I'm not even a Dave Ramsey. To be honest, my checkbook is probably messier than yours, but it seems to me that these scenarios are rather common. Millions of Americans are racking up enormous amounts of debt, and are refusing to forestall any immediate gratification, making expenditures that will haunt them for years. Not only is this bad for our economy in the long run, it teaches our children a very poor lesson in fiscal responsibility. Speaking of poor lessons in fiscal responsibility, let's look at our politicians. Both of our major parties behave irresponsibly when it comes to incurring debt. Romans 13:8 says, *"Let no debt remain outstanding, except the continuing debt to love one another, for whoever loves others has fulfilled the law."*

Do we have many individuals in government today who subscribe to this view on debt? Or was Ronald Reagan right when he said, "Government is like a baby: An alimentary canal with a big appetite at one end and no sense of responsibility at the other."[64] The debt that our children and grandchildren will face due to short-sighted and power-hungry politicians is hardly loving. These "kick the can down the road" weenies will no doubt assert that they are actually spending all of this money for the *good* of future generations. Politicians on both sides of the aisle insist that the debt that *they* vote for is *good* debt. One man's pork is another man's necessity.

Necessity...is it necessary for the good of their constituents or necessary to *buy* votes? The following words have been attributed by some to Alexander Tytler; some attribute them to Alexis de Tocqueville; still others contend that neither gentleman said them. Regardless of *who* said them, they are very profound:

> "A democracy cannot exist as a permanent form of government. It can only exist until the voters discover that they can vote themselves largesse from the public treasury. From that moment on, the majority always votes for the candidates promising the most benefits from the public treasury with the result that a democracy always collapses over loose fiscal policy, always followed by a dictatorship."[65]

Wow, that was a mouthful! As much as I believe these words to be timelessly prophetic, please don't rely on me to critique or dissect this assertion. However, I do know someone who is very knowledgeable about the hearts of men (our politicians), and knows very well whether or not the money they spend (*our* money), is being used to further His Kingdom. Ask God for wisdom and He will tell you whose motives are noble and whose are suspect. When one pays attention to the issues and actually reads the contents of any given bill (something a lot of our representatives can't seem to find the time to do), it becomes a lot easier to discern between responsible uses for tax dollars and frivolous ones.

Once we compare the meat of any given bill to what God has to say about it, we become very dangerous to those representatives who want to continue to spend with reckless abandon. In order to have any credibility when it comes to holding our representatives feet to the fire in the area of spending, we must get our own fiscal houses in order. It makes no sense at all to run your home in a fiscally irresponsible manner and complain when the people you elect to represent you do the very same thing. To wonder why you should be fiscally responsible when our elected officials aren't misses the point. The point is that you know that you answer to God and, sadly, most of them do not. The dangerous thing is that if a politician doesn't care what God says about money, their respect for your concern about how your tax dollars are used is negligible. This type of individual only becomes concerned with responsible spending when their constituents threaten to vote them out of office.

We cannot talk about economics without talking about oppressive taxation.

In order to amass the gargantuan amount of money it takes to either fund legitimate endeavors or insanely frivolous ones, you need to tap the taxpayer on the shoulder and tell them to "cough it up." As previously stated, one man's vitally important program is nonsensical to another, but understanding whether a program is worthy or not in God's eyes is only part of the puzzle. "Reasonable" taxation is a legitimate way to fund endeavors which are necessary to a society's well-being. However, to some, taxation can be a tool to discourage, dispirit, and ultimately crush individuals in order to break them down. Once broken down, they have nowhere to turn but the state.

The economic burden that oppressive taxation puts on average families in this country is staggering. We all seem to be working harder and harder just to keep our heads above water; we're asked to make do with less while our government demands more and more every day. Unlike the aforementioned family who thoughtlessly continues to rack up debt, a lot of Americans are trying very hard to live in a somewhat frugal manner, but they can't seem to maintain the lifestyle they are accustomed to. To some, an easy answer to this is to simply cut back. Although I'm all for individuals managing their finances in a fiscally prudent manner, there's a simpler solution: stop taxing the American people so much!

We are taxed coming and going; morning, noon and night. We are taxed on the federal, state, and local levels. We are taxed so much and in so many ways that even the most simple-minded among us realize that we are being overtaxed. To that point, municipalities and companies have come up with cute little words to mean the same thing as "tax;" words like *impost, duty, fee, assessment, levy, custom, toll,* and *surcharge;* are words that mean the same thing: *tax.* These entities are attempting to soften the verbiage they use when petitioning you to pay a little more than you once did for the same or, oftentimes, lesser service.

One of the most insidious yet predictable outcomes from oppressive taxation is the strain it puts on working mothers. When you ask moms if they would like to stay home and raise their kids (especially from birth to school age), the vast majority would say yes. Although some families flat out refuse to alter their lifestyles once kids are born, a lot more are very willing to scale back economically to enable mom to stay at home and raise the kids. For a lot of families this can't be done regardless of how fiscally responsible they are. The reason is oppressive taxation. Often times, mom has to work just to pay the annual tax bill. Even though half of Americans actually pay no federal income tax, they are still taxed in a myriad of ways, and someone has to pay for that.

Mom is faced with the herculean task of managing the home, educating the kids (not just traditional home school), helping her husband, and about a million other things! She can't realistically do all of these other things well if she can do them at all. What's the result? She and the family are left discouraged, dispirited, and crushed. She has been reduced to a rat on a wheel rather than the wonderful nurturing mother God had intended her to be. I realize every ill in life can't be solved by lowering the tax burden, but a great many problems could indeed be solved by doing just that.

We must keep in mind that economics is not just monetary facts and figures. Many economists espouse economic theory that is highly flawed because they fail to put enough emphasis on the most critical component of any economic analyses: the human being. Fiscal policy that discourages marriage or discourages responsibility in the form of hard work and instead encourages irresponsibility and laziness is the death of any family's, state's, or country's economic system.

A recent Georgia State University study found that many government benefits programs actually discourage people from adopting more productive behaviors. The study's author says, "When the government steps in and subsidizes behaviors that in previous generations would have resulted in great hardship or even death, a sort of social Gresham's Law takes place where bad behavior chases out the good." He goes on to say, "Why have a father and a husband around when the state will assure your financial situation?"[66] To get a good biblical understanding of this let's study one of Paul's warnings to the Thessalonian church. 2 Thessalonians 3:6-15 says:

> *In the name of the Lord Jesus Christ, we command you, brothers and sisters, to keep away from every believer who is idle and disruptive and does not live according to the teaching*

you received from us. For you yourselves know how you ought to follow our example. We were not idle when we were with you, nor did we eat anyone's food without paying for it. On the contrary, we worked night and day, laboring and toiling so that we would not be a burden to any of you. We did this, not because we do not have the right to such help, but in order to offer ourselves as a model for you to imitate. For even when we were with you, we gave you this rule: The one who is unwilling to work shall not eat. We hear that some among you are idle and disruptive. That are not busy; they are busybodies. Such people we command and urge in the Lord Jesus Christ to settle down and earn the food they eat. And as for you, brothers and sisters, never tire of doing what is good. Take special note of anyone who does not obey our instruction in this letter. Do not associate with them, in order that they may feel ashamed. Yet do not regard them as an enemy, but warn them as you would a fellow believer.

Wow, could you just image those words being uttered by any politician in a debate? Of course not. That's why we have such a lack of actual leaders in politics today. Most politicians do not want to be perceived as mean spirited and we live in a society where insistence on productivity is synonymous with mean spiritedness.

Sadly, many politicians have a vested interest in suppressing our economy. Since the beginning of time, this fact is certain: a society's economy is as healthy as the citizens who participate in that society. If individuals become slothful and demanding, either due to their own selfishness or due to the destruction or manipulation of a well-functioning economic structure, the end result is always the same: the government swoops in to save the day. This is why power-hungry politicians actually have a vested interest in our economy doing poorly. God knows what they are up to, and in the end He will judge them for it.

Even though Paul's words are straight from the Bible, a lot of people, including devout believers, take issue with his words of admonishment toward the Thessalonians. Paul is addressing members of the church who felt Christ's return was imminent, so they took this time of expectation to kick back and relax. They stopped being productive. No doubt, there were probably a fair number of others within the church who were opportunists, merely using Christ's promised return as an excuse to be lazy. These types of individuals are among us today and are growing in alarming numbers. They are not opting out of this thing called responsibility because of Christ's imminent return; they have merely come up with a myriad of reasons to sit back and let someone else foot the bill.

It is not necessary to record all of the reasons one may have come up with to arrive at such a flawed way of looking at work. However, I do think it is helpful to look at Paul's words in verse seven to get to the bottom of how this thought process may have started. Paul says, *"For you yourselves know how you ought to fol-low our example."* Paul is speaking to those who were taught the biblical principles of work yet have fallen away from them. Many in this country were taught these things very clearly in church or at least by their parents or teachers when they were growing up. They know deep down in their hearts that what they're doing is wrong, yet they look around and see a world that doesn't seem to subscribe to these principles. Rather than get back to foundational principles, they choose to come up with convenient excuses for their laziness. Even more troubling is an ever-growing segment of our populous that never had these truths instilled in them in the first place. This is where we see fourth and fifth generations that see no problem whatsoever with taking money and services and expecting someone else to pay for them.

The problem with this dynamic is that eventually we will run out of other people's money. If you're offended or angry with my rhetoric, let me calm you down by clearly stating who I am talking about when I refer to the lazy or the slothful. I'm talking about people who are of reasonably sound mind, able-bodied, often-times fairly young who have been blessed with time, treasures, and talents from God. They are the ones who can do many tasks that will yield income, yet they simply refuse to do them. In many countries and, sadly, in ever-growing numbers in our own country, it's simply easier to enjoy many creature comforts by doing nothing instead of working (even a little bit). Politicians figured out a long time ago that it is to their advantage to forward destructive economic policy and then feign an interest in fixing the economic mess that *they* created.

Their disingenuous solution to this mess is always to implement Robin Hood politics which means exactly what it sounds like: taking from the rich and giving to the poor. Proponents of this policy should heed Moses's words in Leviticus 19:15: "*Do not pervert justice; do not show partiality to the poor or favoritism to the great, but judge your neighbor fairly.*" If the poor they were pretending to be concerned about were actually incapable of providing for themselves, I would be somewhat okay with this, but this is often not the case.

These politicians want to *create* an entire society of idle individuals who submit to their rules and regulations. This is done purely and simply to buy votes. Once someone has been defeated, discouraged, and dispirited long enough, they will opt for the path of least resistance which means willingness and, dare I say, eagerness to embrace government largesse. If the large majority of citizens (being encouraged or incentivized by their government) find it more profitable to take rather than produce, that country's economy will simply buckle under such strain.

Paul's words in verse fourteen may seem harsh, as he tells the church to disassociate itself from these idle individuals in order that they may feel ashamed of their behavior. As a culture, we have lost touch with the benefits of shame. It is much easier to feel shame for wrong behavior when the behavior you are engaged in is glaringly odd in comparison to the conduct of everyone else. Years ago, if you were young, able-bodied, of reasonably sound mind and you weren't working (even a little bit), you stuck out like a sore thumb. Today, you are celebrated! Your inability to provide for yourself or your family is simply not your fault. But what if it *is* your fault? Is there anyone besides the Apostle Paul who is pointing that out?

In this politically-correct world, we are afraid to talk about the fact that the emperor is naked. One of the reasons that Christians don't engage in the brotherly admonishment that Paul requires in verse fifteen is because we are afraid of being mischaracterized as cruel and heartless. The media and our politicians contort the rhetoric of those fundamental Christians, misstating what they say as cruel and insensitive as it pertains to those of us who are "idle." Many fundamental Christians don't need anyone to make them look stupid, as their admonishment of the idle *is* cruel and insensitive as it is not motivated by Christlike love.

For example, how do we view the unemployed in this country? For the latter group, it's quite simple: if you don't work, you don't eat. End of discussion. This is hardly displaying Christlike love. There are several factors beyond the control of the average American wage earner that we must take into consideration when understanding our unemployment problem. Corporate downsizing as a result of poor management, the advent of cheap labor abroad or from illegal immigration, and a dearth of job creation due to confiscatory taxation and regulation are but a few of the reasons our country's unemployment rate has stayed high.

Simply put, there are a number of Americans who would like to work but simply can't find jobs. Obviously Paul is not referring to them, and our compassion and understanding of their plight should be on our hearts. These individuals combined with the aforementioned "idle" among us, comprise the current rate of unemployed in this country (roughly 5% as of this writing). However, this figure is woefully suspect as it is in a government's best interest to skew this number, particularly when that government either intentionally or unintentionally creates a poor economic climate through failed policy.

Back when economies were largely cyclical and could limp along or flourish under good or bad governance, it was charitable, yet reasonable, to extend unemployment benefits for 26 weeks. For a whole host of good and bad reasons, these benefits have now been extended to 99 weeks. The points to be considered about two years of government subsidy is that the longer someone is not a productive wage earner, the more discouraged and dispirited the person becomes and the drive to return to the workforce diminishes every day. This is devastating to our economy, our families, and the individual for a whole host of obvious reasons.

This phenomenon should be quite apparent to anyone. The next phenomenon may not be. The unemployment subsidy (whether you feel it's fair or not) must eventually cease. Now what? Is that person no longer unemployed? A dumb question, you may say, or is it? A rapidly growing segment of our population is no longer eligible for unemployment insurance.

Let's go back to the 5% unemployment rate. The US Bureau of Labor Statistics releases two unemployment rates. The first one is the U3 report which measures individuals who are out of a job and are *currently looking for work*. The second report is the U6 report which includes the aforementioned individuals *and* an ever-growing group who, for one reason or another, has *stopped looking for work*. The U6 report also includes the underemployed who have lost their full-time job, would like to work full-time, but have been forced to take a part-time job. If most of the individuals in the U6 group are clearly unemployed, then why aren't they being counted in the unemployment number? Are they no longer unemployed? Just ask the wife or children of a man who has been unemployed for two years and listen to what they tell you. If the *true* unemployment figures (the ones that include these individuals) were ever reported, they would probably be closer to 14%.[67] This is shameful. If this accurate figure were to be reported, it would shine a glaring spotlight on many of the flawed policies that led to this catastrophe. That's why the numbers reflected in the U6 report never get reported.

If we want to see where all this is headed, we don't need a crystal ball, we just have to look at what's happening in Greece. Greek voters, by an astounding 61% to 38%, rejected demands by international creditors for more austerity measures in exchange for yet another bailout of its bankrupt economy. Austerity measures are simply attempts to significantly curtail government spending in an effort to control public sector debt, especially when a nation is in jeopardy of defaulting on its bonds. To put it simply, don't keep spending what you don't have. In the past, this was a concept that almost everyone on the planet understood; today it's unfortunately a foreign concept to a lot of people. This blatant obliviousness to a basic economic tenet doesn't happen overnight. It's permitted and, dare I say, cultivated over time resulting in what we see happening in Greece today. Prime Minister Alexis Tsipras campaigned and was elected on a promise to repeal bailout austerity. Bailout austerity is a lender saying, "We'll continue to loan you money but you must show us that you are implementing belt-tightening policies to get yourself out of this mess." You would think that Greece would be unbelievably grateful that anyone would be willing to help them given the attitude of most of their leaders and an even greater number of its citizens, but you would be wrong. In the face of an international bailout of 240 billion euros expiring, and the country defaulting on an IMF repayment (the first developed nation ever to do so), what was Greece's response? A lopsided vote indicating loudly and clearly to the world that the Greek people will not alter their lifestyles in any way, shape, manner, or form and oh, by the way, keep the money rolling in, will ya? This insanity was best summed up by Prime Minister Tsipras himself as he stated that, "We proved that even in the most difficult circumstances that democracy won't be blackmailed."[68] Huh?!? Syndicated radio talk show host Pat Gray said it best when he said, "When your credit card company calls you up and demands their money, try telling them that democracy won't be blackmailed!"

The sad reality is that there is safety in numbers. The Greek people are confident that if enough of them simply refuse to be productive, the government won't possibly cut them all off. Unfortunately it looks like they're right. Lest you think I'm being too hard on the Greeks, let's briefly look at what's going in in that country. The Greek government is wrought with corruption. Patronage jobs and sweet deals for friends and family are just the way the government operates. Government jobs pay three times as much as private-sector jobs. Greek public schools have the lowest ranking in Europe despite four times greater funding than the number-one ranked public school system. The Greek government will allow you to retire at 50 (women), 55 (men) if you have an arduous job. Because everyone wants to kick back and take, the government has now categorized hair dressers, waiters, and radio talk-show hosts, among other vocations, as arduous. If you are ambitious enough or, some might say, foolish enough to actually work in Greece, you are allotted an unimaginable amount of vacation time. During these holidays, the country is even more unproductive than it normally is. Unemployment is through the roof and the number of Greeks who are disabled (or at least claim to be) dwarfs any other population on the planet. The average person doesn't even bother to pay taxes and if they know someone in high places, they don't have to worry about any repercussions. All in all, if the majority of a society's citizens have palms on both sides of their hands, that society's economy will collapse.

We've discussed personal and national debt as well as oppressive taxation, but we cannot fully understand economics without discussing tithing. The tithe is simply the contribution of one tenth of one's income to the church. There are some minor variances to this principle, but the aforementioned definition is all you need to know in order to understand the principle. If you're not a Christian or a respecter of biblical principles, tithing makes no sense at all.

Years ago I had a friend who was an accountant and a member of a local church, but he was more "religious" than "Christian." Because of his propensity for number crunching, the elder board thought it would be a good idea to recruit him to get the church's finances in order. After a few meetings, it was easy to see what was most important to him. He felt it was insane to ask financially strapped parishioners to tithe, to give *more* on Sunday, when they were having trouble paying their own bills. He failed to realize the truth of Psalm 24:1: "*The earth is the Lord's, and everything in it, the world, and all who live in it.*"

Sadly, most of our churches today are filled with folks who are just "playing" at Christianity. They go through the motions of the whole "religious" thing, but they never seem to get any deeper than a peripheral relationship with God or His principles. Tithing is a bizarre concept to anyone who sees it in strictly monetary terms. There are several reasons to tithe, but I feel that the following are the most important:

1) We should tithe because we realize that that the money we earn is *first* God's money. He has graciously allowed us to earn it, but despite our efforts, it's still His. He only asks for a dime out of every dollar. Given the fact that He has provided us with the ability and opportunity to earn money, it only makes sense to acknowledge this by giving Him the first fruits of our labor. This first reason fits into the *reverence and awe* category.

2) After we establish a healthy fear of the Lord for who He is and what He has done, we realize a second reason to tithe: to show our love and appreciation for God. He blesses us daily in more ways than we can imagine. Once we start counting our blessings, we become truly thankful for what He has lovingly bestowed upon us. We start to understand how much He loves us, and we, in turn, show our love back to Him by giving Him 10% of our income.

3) Lastly, once we revere Him and are thankful to Him, we can start to experience the true cause-and-effect of the biblical principle of tithing. Malachi 3:10 says:

> *"Bring the whole tithe into the storehouse, that there be food in my house. Test me in this, says the Lord Almighty, and see if I will not throw open the floodgates of heaven and pour out so much blessing that there will not be enough to store it."*

What my accountant friend never understood was that wealth was first created by God and *then* graciously bestowed upon us. Furthermore, the management of that wealth is of great importance to our creator. Our country, its business community, and particularly its citizens, should always employ sound economic doctrine in whatever they do in order to have a chance at returning to greatness. However, if our priorities are not in the right order, God will not bless us in the overflowing way that He desires. We need only to heed the words of Matthew (someone who knew a fair amount about money) when he said in Matthew 6:21, *"For where your treasure is, there your heart will be also."* He went on to say in Matthew 6:33, *"But seek first his kingdom and his righteousness, and all these things will be given to you as well."*

America is a capitalistic society, and to many capitalism is a dirty word. Believe it or not, I have a family member who is a born-again Christian with many Marxist beliefs! I don't get it either, but I roll with it. During a recent discussion about free-market capitalism, he was both heartened and surprised when I said, "Capitalism is indeed a much-failed system as the rich get richer and the poor get poorer *if there isn't a reverence for God Almighty* at best, and a healthy respect for the rule of law at least. There are plenty of places in the world where capitalism is practiced without either of those things and, yes, the poor would be better off in a more socialistic society. *However,* when capitalism is practiced with those principles in mind, it is the greatest promoter of people in *every* socioeconomic group."

RESHAPING AMERICA

John Mackey, CEO of Whole Foods, has set out to dispel the myth that capitalism is based upon unethical principles such as greed, selfishness, and exploitation. Mr. Mackey contends that "Business is the greatest value creator in the world. Business creates value for its customers, its employees, its suppliers, for its investors, for the larger communities…we are the value creators."[69] Mr. Mackey is correct: business, in general, should not be vilified but rather encouraged to flourish in order to benefit everyone. Many thoughtful economists embrace a form of trickle-down economics, whereby the shackles of burdensome taxation are lessened in order to stimulate economic growth. Lessening the tax burden on higher-income individuals encourages them to lay out risk capital rather than hoard their assets. The result? Poorer members of society benefit as the whole economy improves. As John F. Kennedy used to say, "A rising tide lifts all boats."

I think you get the point by now that our economy cannot flourish separate and apart from God's blessing. How do we set ourselves up for His favor? Obey God's principles. It's as simple as that. David Brat, an economics professor at Randolph Macon College, catapulted to the national stage as a result of his David-and-Goliath victory over House Majority Leader Eric Cantor in a Republican primary for the US House of Representatives. Jeff Kearns of Bloomberg writes, "David Brat's economic dashboard is more like a moral compass. Mr. Brat sees virtue as the foundation for U.S. economic gains."[70]

Webster's defines virtue as, "Moral excellence and righteousness; goodness." These are hardly terms that many Americans associate with the drivers of our economy, but these forces are nonetheless essential in order for our economy to prosper. Mr. Brat said, "Economists are slow to acknowledge perhaps the most powerful institution in Western civilization: religion."[71] Will he ultimately be demonized for suggesting that we mix a little religion with our country's economic policies? Probably. But it doesn't matter. People who think like Mr. Brat are demonized and mischaracterized whether they speak up or not.

ACTION STEPS

1. Study the Bible to find out what God says about money.

2, Ask yourself: Is my economic house in order?

3. Find out how the politicians who represent you allocate your tax dollars.

4. Pray for wisdom before you talk to your family or friends about money.

5. Pray for God's wisdom when deciding how to handle the money with which He blesses you.

8

ObamaCare

Although we've discussed abortion and euthanasia, topics which sadly fall into the category of "health care," I'd like to take this opportunity to talk about health care in general; specifically, the Patient Protection and Affordable Care Act, better known as ObamaCare. I realize that talking about this massive 2,700 page overhaul of our health care system is risky business. The eyes of the average citizen glaze over quickly when anyone attempts to explain the various aspects of this law. However, we should at least acquaint ourselves with its basic tenets and what they mean for our country. It's a daunting task, given that none other than House Minority Leader Nancy Pelosi declared that "We'll have to pass the bill *first* so that you can find out what's in it." If one of the most important legislators in the land can't even take the time to read the bill, a case could be made for giving the average citizen a pass when it comes to their knowledge of ObamaCare.

The general motivation for ObamaCare was to make sure that the whopping 48 million Americans (15% of our nation), who do not have health care, have access to health care. Before we start, let's identify who those 48 million people are. Right off the top, twelve million (a conservative estimate) are illegal aliens.[72] I'm not suggesting that we deny these individuals emergent or urgent medical care, but factoring them into the health care debate puts the cart before the horse.

Why are these individuals included in the 48 million figure? Is it because people really care about them and want to see them have affordable health care? Or is because including them helps further a cause?

Next there are eighteen million Americans who are between the ages of 18 and 34 who, for the most part, *choose* not to have health care. Whether or not you think that's foolish is beside the point. They're adults and they can decline to have funds taken out of their paychecks to fund their health care. Secondly, whether these individuals are clueless or thoughtful, the fact of the matter is that their decision to decline health insurance is a safe statistical bet. Individuals in this age group are, for the most part, the healthiest in our country. If they want to keep more money in their pockets until they actually *need* health insurance, that's their right. Compelling them or any other demographic to buy health insurance is un-American, regardless of the Supreme Court's tortured logic on the matter.

Transcending all demographics is a group of fourteen million who are indeed eligible for Medicaid or State Children's Health Insurance Program (SCHIP) programs, yet have never taken the time to enroll. When they do enter the system, they are encouraged to enroll in these programs, but many, for one reason or another, neglect to do so.

Oddly enough, the fastest growing segment of the uninsured population (eighteen million) are individuals who earn in excess of $50,000 annually, and half of them earn more than $75,000 annually. Again, this group has determined that they will, for at least the time being, remain uninsured. It would be inaccurate to simply add up the numbers of each of these groups to prove a point, as many would be counted multiple times as they fit into several categories. However, when we actually take a critical look at the number of Americans who would like to have affordable health care and cannot obtain it, the smoke clears and the 48 million number plummets to about eight million individuals. That's only 3% of our population.

Why do I devote so much space to illustrate the real number of uninsured Americans? To assert that a complete overhaul of the greatest health care system in the world for 3% of our population is madness, especially when the changes take us from the frying pan to the fire. When you have some remodeling to do to your kitchen, you call a kitchen remodeler; you don't take a wrecking ball to your whole house.

ObamaCare is unequivocally the biggest thing that will reshape America for decades to come. As I have said, God is more concerned with our hearts than with our actions. Proverbs 27:19 says, *"As water reflects the face, so one's life reflects the heart."* The details of ObamaCare, with which I think even Nancy Pelosi is now familiar, are important, but the motivation behind ObamaCare is of much greater significance.

Opinions run the gamut. Some think our health care system was dysfunctional and broken and left too many citizens vulnerable. They agree that a complete overhaul of the system was necessary in order to best serve everyone. Its complete and utter transformation was just what the doctor ordered, and they enthusiastically welcome sweeping changes. Others believe that we have by far the best health care system in the world, and it only needed to be improved upon, not overhauled. Many with this mindset have even gone so far as to suggest that ObamaCare has much more to do with a grander plan to expand government and stifle individual rights.

I believe that before we explore those views, we must first study the architects of ObamaCare. Once we understand who these individuals are, we can get a better working understanding of *why* they came up with the various aspects of ObamaCare.

The colossally bloated cost of $650 million to construct the HealthCare.Gov website was shameful. The myriad of technical glitches visitors to the website encountered were frustrating, embarrassing, and yet thoroughly predictable. The emotional tumult that the insurance industry is being put through illustrates very clearly the devastating result of an intrusive, overreaching government cluelessly, yet forcefully, wading into free market areas. As a result of this meddling, millions of Americans have been irreparably harmed financially and, sadly, physically. The worst part is that ObamaCare has not even hit its stride yet. These things are proof enough that this ill-fated monstrosity will radically change our country for the worse. However, because of laziness, apathy, ignorance, and naïveté, some people need more proof that a government takeover of the finest healthcare system in the world might not be such a good idea.

Enter the V.A. scandal. We have a crystal-clear foreshadowing of what government-provided health care will be like when we look at the recent VA scandal. To subject the bravest and most honorable among us to a health care system that barely exceeds third world medical care is unconscionable. I know first-hand that all the horrible things that we have heard about in the VA are not really news at all. These atrocities have been going on for decades; they only came to light because a few brave VA employees decided to speak out. Despite being routinely warned by their superiors not to talk to the media, they did the right thing and refused to be silent. We should be indebted to these individuals for their courage.

You really didn't have to be a VA employee to figure out that something was terribly amiss in this system. Anyone with even casual knowledge of it was well aware of the frightful conditions and substandard care delivered by bungling, incompetent bureaucrats.[73] How's that for a thanks for serving our country?

Early opponents of ObamaCare warned of rationed healthcare due to doctor shortages, administrative incompetence and fraud, denied services due to nameless and faceless bureaucrats deciding who is worthy and who is not, lack of diagnostic services, delayed and, ultimately, substandard care. The VA mess encompasses all of these things and is a clear warning of what we will all face soon enough.

ObamaCare, aside from incompetence and inefficiency, forces businesses to provide all Food and Drug Administration-approved contraceptive methods for eligible women through their health insurance plans. The government does grant some "religious employers" an exemption to this mandate. Unfortunately the government didn't seem to think that Hobby Lobby, a chain of merchandise stores, qualified for this exemption. Hobby Lobby sued the federal government on the grounds that some of the contraceptive drugs or devices have the potential to terminate life.

Drugs or devices that prevent fertilization of an egg are not in question here; it's the drugs/devices (abortifacients) that prevent a fertilized egg (better known as a human life) from implanting in a woman's uterus that the owners of the company have a problem with. The company is owned by the Green family, who has publicly declared that they have always run their company according to their gospel convictions. They close their stores on Sundays and have a faith statement in their company charter.

The Supreme Court in a 5-4 ruling decided that Hobby Lobby qualifies for an exemption to the contraceptive mandate. In order to be granted an exemption, a company must prove that they have sincere religious conviction, which has been consistently demonstrated through the history of the company. They must also prove that the mandate substantially burdens their religious faith. Regardless of what the Supreme Court decided, the ultimate judge sits in a much higher seat and He will not be mocked.

Unfortunately, this mandate and the monstrosity that is ObamaCare, never had to happen in the first place. Enter into the picture Bart Stupak. Bart Stupak was a Democrat congressman from the state of Michigan. He was a pro-life Democrat, or at least some thought so. At the time, ObamaCare was inching ever closer to being the law of the land, but it needed a few more votes in Congress to make it a reality. A presumed pro-life congressman, Bart Stupak was the last deciding vote to drag ObamaCare over the finish line.

Stupak committed to voting for ObamaCare after he received assurances from President Obama that he would personally intervene and sign an executive order protecting the Hyde amendment (bill S.142) which was introduced on 1/24/13 by Senator Robert P. Casey Jr. (D) PA. The explanation of the bill is as simple as it gets: to prohibit the expenditure of Federal funds for abortions, and for other purposes.[74] Pro-life critics said an executive order was not worth the paper it was written on, as President Obama could just as easily undo this order at a later date. The prestigious Susan B. Anthony organization, an organization that seeks to end abortion, stripped Mr. Stupak of the "Defender of Life Award" they had bestowed upon him as a result of his sell out vote on ObamaCare.

Executive Director Marjorie Dannenfelser said, "Let me be clear: any representative, including Representative Stupak, who votes for this health care bill can no longer call themselves pro-life."[75] Her organization halted plans to help Mr. Stupak get reelected to Congress, and he dropped out of the race shortly thereafter, retiring from politics altogether. Subsequently, the Health and Human Services Department has indeed mandated that taxpayers certainly do have to fund contraception, including abortion inducing drugs. This mandate led Hobby Lobby to make a stand. Praise God that they won.[76]

As if ObamaCare has not taken enough hits since its inception, add the condescending yet revealing comments of one of its key architects and it's a wonder that this monstrosity still stands. Here is just one of several comments MIT economist Jonathan Gruber has made about ObamaCare: "Lack of transparency is a huge political advantage and basically, call it the stupidity of the American voter or whatever, basically that was really critical to getting the thing to pass."[77]

It might seem odd for someone to admit the need for deception in crafting and marketing ObamaCare, and then in the same breath call the people he is trying to fool stupid. If they are so stupid, why do you need to fool them? Permit me to clarify Mr. Gruber's seemingly contradictory comments. The Obama Administration's desire to be less than transparent with the true design and intent of ObamaCare was necessary to avoid "waking up" a sizable segment of the populous. These individuals are much more ignorant or apathetic than they are "stupid." It was critical that they remain asleep during the ObamaCare debate in order to get the bill passed.

According to Gruber, the best way to do that was to be "less than transparent" or, in layman's terms, lie about the details of ObamaCare. Perhaps the more appropriate word to describe the masses Mr. Gruber felt the need to dupe would be *gullible*. This is actually more disturbing, as a country of gullible individuals is even more dangerous than a country of stupid individuals.

The plot thickened as key players in ObamaCare, Speaker of the House Nancy Pelosi and President Obama himself, claimed not to even know Jonathan Gruber. Mr. Gruber went from being referred to as the "architect of ObamaCare" and a "go-to expert," to being called "some advisor" once the firestorm started. Unfortunately for them, the same Google searches that have exposed Mr. Gruber very quickly exposed Obama's and Pelosi's claims as well. Shortly after Speaker Pelosi said that she didn't know who Mr. Gruber was and that he didn't write the bill, it was discovered that she cited him specifically in a 2009 speech, lauding his favorable analyses of ObamaCare.

Similarly, in the heat of the controversy, President Obama referred to Mr. Gruber as "some advisor who was never on our staff." However, this "obscure" advisor, while technically not on the White House staff, did receive a cool $400,000 for his technical analyses of the bill. Additionally, in a 2006 speech at the Brookings Institute, then-Senator Obama referred to Gruber as one of the sharpest minds in academia and admits to "liberally" stealing ideas (interesting adverb) from him and other bright minds. One of those other bright minds that President Obama admits to stealing from is Jim Wallis who he says can inform what are sometimes dry policy debates with a "prophetic voice." This man with a "prophetic voice" is a huge proponent of socialized medicine.

Eventually, sooner or later, every single one of us will need health care. Controlling the health care system is the grand prize for any leftist. If the state can worm its way into every aspect of health care, the game is simply over. Once you control an individual's health, you have them in the palm of your hand and they'll forego all kinds of freedoms just for the flickering hope that the state will graciously and beneficently "promise to take care of" their health care needs.

We as believers know that one's spiritual health trumps everything else. But for the purposes of this discussion, let's assume that without one's physical health, most things in life come to a screeching halt. With that in mind, it's chilling to imagine what will happen if the state can control who practices health care, where they practice, how they practice, what fees they can charge for services, who qualifies for health care, and more appropriately, who *doesn't.*

America is a God-fearing and compassionate society that truly cares about its citizens. The left in this country, through ObamaCare, seeks to exploit our innate kind-heartedness. They assert that the ultimate arbiter of compassion, the federal government, is best equipped to do that. Christian leftists such as Jim Wallis correctly assert that a society is measured by how it treats its most vulnerable citizens. As previously stated, I pray these Christian leftists would be a little more concerned with the epitome of the most vulnerable (the unborn), but we can only hope. The remainder of the most vulnerable in our society—those fortunate enough to have been birthed—are admittedly not thriving, but they are certainly recipients of the finest health care that the world has ever provided.

Mr. Wallis asserts that the United States should move toward a more just system of providing health care and that the state is just the entity to do it, a noble goal which he claims is backed up by Scripture.[78] The elephant in the room is the fact that the Bible never says that society and the state are one and the same. In America, our society comprises well-meaning Christian (and non-Christian) citizens, various charitable organizations, religious organizations of every stripe, nuclear families, extended families, and amalgamations of all sorts of compassionate people.

The state, even as it exists in a relatively free society such as ours, is certainly *not* who God has in mind when it comes to devising and disseminating quality health care. Its bloody history of state-sanctioned murder (abortion), infanticide in dogged opposition to the Born-Alive Infants Protection Act, fierce opposition to parental notification of minors seeking abortions, and widespread support of doctor assisted-suicide (euthanasia), are just some of the myriad reasons why the health of our citizens can never be entrusted to such an entity.

The successful demagoguing of the phrase "death panel" has served the left well throughout the ObamaCare debate. At first blush, no rational American citizen could possibly fathom that their government would be in the business of deciding in a Roman-style, thumbs-up/thumbs-down manner, who lives or dies. It's positively un-American, right? You're darn right it is. However, these Independent Payment Advisory Boards (IPABs) have tremendous unconstitutional power and can very easily operate free from any oversight from the three branches of government, all in the name of "affordable" health care.

It's naïve and dangerous to think that many of the decisions that these panels will make on who gets what health care and when will not result in a person living or dying; common sense tells us that it most certainly will. At the end of the day, you don't need to be an expert in health care to know that giving the power of life and, regrettably, death to fifteen unelected bureaucrats with very strong ideological ties to our president is Orwellian.

Finally, the Supreme Court has ruled 5-4 (King vs. Burwell) to uphold the outlay of tax credits to qualifying persons in all states, both those with exchanges established directly by a state, and those otherwise established by the Department of Health and Human Services. An exchange is an online marketplace for health insurance. ObamaCare opponents contended that the plain language of the statute provided eligibility for tax credits only to those persons in states with state-operated exchanges. The majority of the Court rejected this stating, "Congress made the guaranteed issue and community rating requirements applicable in every State in the Nation. But those requirements only work when combined with the coverage requirement and tax credits. So it stands to reason that Congress meant for those provisions to apply in every state as well."[79] As was the case with the same-sex marriage ruling the following day, the latest decision by the Supreme Court had very little to do with law and almost everything to do with an unquenchable desire to forward an agenda. As you might imagine, Judge Antonin Scalia had plenty to say about what he perceives as a runaway court bent on legislating from the bench, saying, "...[T]his Court's two decisions on the Act will surely be remembered through the years. The somersaults of statutory interpretation they have performed ('penalty' means tax, 'further [Medicaid] payments to the State' means only incremental Medicaid payments to the State, 'established by the State' means not established by the State) will be cited by litigants endlessly, to the confusion of honest jurisprudence. And the cases will publish forever the discouraging truth that the Supreme Court of the United States favors some laws over others, and is prepared to do whatever it takes to uphold and assist its favorites." In commenting on the painstaking lengths that the Court has taken to "revise" ObamaCare in terms of authorizing the IRS to spend tens of billions of dollars every year in tax credits in federal exchanges, Scalia said, "The legislature not only commands the purse but prescribes the rules by which the duties and rights of every citizen are to be regulated. The judiciary on the contrary, has no influence over… the purse; no direction… of the wealth of a society, and can take no active resolution whatever. It may truly be said to have neither FORCE nor WILL but merely judgment."[80]

At the crux of both the same-sex marriage ruling and the latest ObamaCare ruling is the dogged determination of most of its judges to "help along" laws they feel should be upheld. This blatant failure to adhere to their judiciary obligation is best summed up, again, by Scalia: "Perhaps sensing the dismal failure of its efforts to show that 'established by the State' means 'established by the State or the Federal Government,' the Court tries to palm off the pertinent statutory phrase as 'inartful drafting.'… this Court, however, has no free floating power to 'rescue Congress from its drafting errors.'"

Lastly, Republican Senator Ted Cruz of Texas had these thoughts on the most recent ObamaCare ruling: "Not only are the Court's opinions untethered from reason and logic, they are also alien to our constitutional system of limited and divided government. By redefining the meaning of common words, and redesigning the most basic human institutions, this Court has crossed from the realm of activism into the area of oligarchy." I agree with Senator Cruz when he says, "Sadly, the political reaction from the leaders of my party is all too predictable.[81] They will pretend to be incensed, and then plan to do absolutely nothing." As I've stated in a previous chapter, Democrats and liberals are not the main problem here! As has been articulated by Judge Scalia, LEGISLATURES control funding! Republicans (you know, the party that tells you they're for God, family, and the American way) are the ones who have numbers in both houses and are doing nothing to choke off funding for this monstrosity. You can't stump for votes at town hall meetings by billing yourself as the "God" party and then act this way. They would do well to heed the words of James 4:17: *If anyone, then, knows the good they ought to do and doesn't do it, it is sin for them.*

ACTION STEPS

1. Try to read the text of the Patient Protection and Affordable Care Act (ObamaCare) or as much of it as you can. Write down any questions that you may have.

2. Research numerous credible sources to try to get those questions answered.

3. Find out what type of people are the architects of ObamaCare. Does their worldview square with the word of God?

4. Find out what your representatives think of ObamaCare and why.

5. Talk to your insurance company and fellow citizens about how ObamaCare affects them.

9

The Family

But at the beginning of creation God made them male and female. For this reason a man will leave his father and mother and be united to his wife, and the two will become one flesh. So they are no longer two but one flesh. Therefore what God has joined together, let no one separate.

—Mark 10:6-9

The family is the bedrock of any civilization, and the inseparable bond between a husband and wife is of vital importance if the family wants to thrive in this broken world. Can there be good families out there without this God-intended dynamic? Of course. The words contained in this chapter are in no way meant to impugn, besmirch, or delegitimize family dynamics that, for one reason or another, don't resemble God's template of a mother and father with their children. There are a whole lot of God-fearing folks who are simply doing the best they can with the situation they're in. However, the message I'd like to convey in this chapter is one of hope in a world where a solid traditional marriage is oftentimes seen as an unattainable fairy tale. There are enough "how to have a great marriage" books out there, so I'm not going to take the time to parrot many of their common-sense philosophies. Instead, I'd like to examine whether or not most forms of cultural decay can be traced back to broken homes.

Just as being a product of a broken home doesn't seal your fate, growing up in a solid traditional Christian home doesn't guarantee a smooth ride. However, the likelihood of becoming all God wants you to be—thereby impacting our country for the good—dramatically increases if you are a product of a solid, two-parent family. The devil knows this, and that's why divorce is a priority for him. The evil one starts early and often, as he poisons young minds about the institution of marriage long before they could even contemplate entering into such a sacred covenant.

Children who are the products of divorce can be very wary of marriage, and often they enter into adulthood filled with cynicism about finding (and staying with) their soulmate. It's no wonder that young people (regardless of their parent's marital status) have such a fretful view of marriage. After all, we know the statistics: half of all marriages end in divorce. Even more sobering is that the same rate applies to Christian and non-Christian marriages alike, right? Maybe not.

Christian author Shaunti Feldhahn felt that those statistics couldn't possibly be accurate, so she set out to debunk them. And debunk them she did! Mrs. Feldhahn found that the demoralizing and discouraging divorce statistics that we've all heard are simply not true. Of particular interest to me was the often-echoed statistic that the divorce rate among Christians is the same (50%) as everyone else. That assertion didn't seem to jibe with what Mrs. Feldhahn and several others in the church were seeing so she worked to try to get a better understanding of those numbers.

What she found was fascinating. The original study was done by the Barna Group. Mrs. Feldhahn learned that they had studied the *beliefs* of the respondents rather than their *actions* as they pertained to their Christianity. The Barna Group came to the conclusion that those who held Christian beliefs had the same divorce rates as those who said they didn't. Mrs. Feldhahn partnered with Barna and reran the numbers, and they found out that when the person was asked if they were in a church the prior week, their divorce rate dropped 27% compared to those who weren't.

Does simply attending church insulate us from divorce? Sadly, no. However, several studies have found that church attendance drops the divorce rate 25-50% compared to those individuals who do not attend church. These and many other hopeful insights on marriage can be found in Shaunti Feldhahn's book, *The Good News About Marriage*. The misunderstanding of the original data has led to a much-skewed view of the divorce rates between believers and non-believers, so we should be grateful to Shaunti Feldhahn for her work in this area.[82]

The bottom line is that actions speak louder than words. A good marriage is not just going to happen; you and your spouse have to work hard and be ever vigilant in this fight. Satan knows that if he breaks up couples he can break up families; if he breaks up families, those families will likely produce wayward children. Those children will often perpetuate the cycle or, at the least, be severely damaged by the devastation of divorce. Their "baggage" may lead them down paths they ought not to travel. Sadly, if enough of these products of collateral damage make up our society, we have a huge problem.

The cultural benefits of married people staying together for a lifetime have been obvious to people throughout history, regardless of faith or lack thereof. Married parents who are *committed* to staying together have a greater chance of developing upstanding, productive human beings than parents who don't see the need to even get married in the first place. It may seem odd to have to tell any rational soul not to put the cart before the horse, but this is not the world we live in.

The backbone of any thriving culture is its citizens' sense of commitment. Are we really "all in?" A society whose citizens are not really "all in" tend to not care about the things one ought to care about. Believing in God Almighty, obeying the rules and laws He set forth, going to church, staying faithful to your spouse, procreating and raising your children to obey and fear God, getting a good education, getting a good job, doing your best at that job, taking care of one's health, making friends, being there for those friends, you get the point. Commitment to God, family, spouse, friends, teammates, employers, co-workers, fellow citizens, and country, in general, is essential for a culture to thrive. When any of these (particularly the first three) start breaking down, a culture ceases to thrive and starts to merely exist.

That type of culture rests on its laurels and starts to cruise on auto-pilot. Fear of God, an appreciation for freedom, willingness to fight for it, and a respect for the rule of law don't just happen. These things have to be understood. A citizen has to believe in their heart that these things are an integral part of society. If they don't, they will have no vested interest in sustaining such principles. This indifference can only go on for a finite period of time before the society starts to crumble.

The average age of any great culture is 200 years.[83] The United States is 239 and, as you can see, we are on borrowed time. When the number of individuals in a society who have no concern for the aforementioned principles starts to exceed and subsequently dwarf the few individuals in that society who actually do care about the things that matter to God, that society is in freefall. Even with an omnipotent God who loves the United States dearly, the task of abating this cultural slide becomes futile. The few who do care simply become tired of fighting the fight and give up. Are we there yet? No, but we are approaching this point at warp speed.

An astounding 41% of all children in the United States are born out of wedlock. (In 1965 that figure was 7%). The percentage balloons up to 72% in the African American community. Sociologists contend that when 25% of society's births are out of wedlock, the fabric of that society starts to tear rapidly.[84] Our society won't have a prayer if these numbers continue to rise. As Shaunti Feldhahn's research tells us, a commitment to God dramatically increases the likelihood that married people will stay together.

But what about a simple commitment to one another, living together first as a logical precursor to marriage? Unfortunately, most individuals who live together before marriage never get married. A cynic would say that this illustrates that a trial run is a good thing, snuffing out relationships before they would have eventually ended in divorce. This is flawed logic.

The latter group is going to be especially hard to turn. For these individuals, commitment to a lifelong spouse is a concept that they are not even willing to ponder for any length of time. Worse than one who is impervious to any debate on the subject is the poor soul who has never even heard the case for a committed marriage. It's bad enough that they may be the product of several generations of ignorance on this matter, but you'd at least hope that someone *outside* their orb would care enough to at least try to stop this madness. The survival of our nation depends on a willingness by individuals, the church, and the state (in that order) to encourage marriage.

Husbands

Its 5:00 and you actually got out of work at a decent hour. Miraculously, you're cruising down the expressway unencumbered. At this rate, you'll probably make it home by 6:00. *You* worked hard today and it's time for *you* to do what *you* wanna do tonight. You imagine how the night will roll out. Your wife has prepared a piping hot, sumptuous meal. Despite the fact that she might want to enjoy this meal at the table as a family, you'd rather perch your plate precariously on your ever-expanding belly as you lie prostrate on the couch watching the pre-game show on ESPN. Next, the big game itself! It should only take about three hours away from the family on a weeknight. And then… you guessed it… it's time for a little lovin'. You have a great night planned because after all, you deserve it!

Unfortunately, and unbeknown to you, there's another party involved here: your wife. Her day has not gone so smoothly. Her part-time job is starting to require full-time hours. The lunch that she scheduled so she could counsel a hurting friend and the meeting with the math teacher of your struggling third-grader simply had to be blown off due to a lack of time. When she arrived home she was greeted by a sink full of dirty dishes, a basket of dirty clothes only feet away from the washing machine, a voicemail from a bill collector, and three disrespectful and very hungry kids demanding to know what's for dinner. Meanwhile, your little third-grader slumps over his math book mumbling about how dumb he is for doing so poorly in class.

This is a train wreck waiting to happen. Mom is spinning, wondering what to do first. She loads the washing machine and the dishwasher as she attempts to console her hurting son. All the while her two fully capable teenage girls wail on and on about their hunger pangs. This is when you enter, with one thing on your mind: you. As you side-step the remaining dirty clothes in the basket on the floor and cavalierly saunter past your struggling son, you triumphantly assume your rightful position on the couch and cluelessly yell to your wife, "Call me when dinner's ready." There is literally steam coming out of your wife's ears, but because she has made it a point to meditate on Ephesians 5:22-24 for years, she remains silent. Since she is human, she can't help but wonder "does he not see the dirty dishes, dirty clothes, struggling kid, insolent ungrateful teenagers, no food in sight and it's well after 6:00? Is he that blind, insensitive, dim witted, etc.?"

While you enjoy your "rights" as a husband to hours of manly television watching, your wife dutifully performs all the mundane tasks that are part of being a mom and a wife. Still oblivious, you figure "I got some good TV watchin', I got a great meal, in front of the BIG screen so as not to be distracted by the family…why not go for the trifecta?" You guessed it: you want a little lovin' before you go to bed. Why shouldn't you want this? After all, Paul wouldn't have said to the Ephesians, "*Now as the church submits to Christ, so also wives should submit to their husbands in everything,*" if it weren't important.

So that fateful time has arrived: 10:00 PM. He wants a little, *you know,* and all she can do is pray for some degree of calm in her home until sleep mercifully sets in. Because she's a woman and she deals with crap 24/7, she has the incredible ability to stuff, forget, or hopefully give up to the Lord all the craziness that has happened today. But this dynamic is about to change as her knuckle-dragging oaf of a husband is going to press his luck. This isn't going to be pretty. As she makes her way to her side of the bed, you give her "that look," and she shoots back a look of her own.

I can guarantee you that those looks mean vastly different things. His look means "I want my needs met, so what do you say?" Her look is a twisted, tortured amalgamation of rage, frustration, and bewilderment. She thinks, "Is he really that clueless?" He thinks nothing of the suggestion. And then it happens. They start talking, then the talking leads to arguing, then the arguing leads to fighting and things get really ugly. He ends up sleeping on that couch he loves (ironic, isn't it?), and she cries herself to sleep wondering why their marriage is so out of whack.

Sound familiar? It does if you're honest. The sad thing is that this didn't have to happen. If the guy had been meditating on Ephesians 5:25 as long as his wife had been meditating on Ephesians 5:22-24, this fight could have been averted.

So what is the husband's role in reshaping America? First, his priorities should be the same as every other citizen: to meditate on Mark 12:30, which says to *"Love the Lord your God with all your heart and with all your soul and with all your mind and with all your strength."* By committing to obey this simple commandment, the husband will experience a sense of honor and duty to his God, wife, children, and community to be the best he can be. As a byproduct, America will become a better place. Secondly, with God's help, he should commit to executing Ephesians 5:25 to the best of his ability: *"Husbands, love your wives as Christ loved the church and gave himself up for her."* A tall order, no doubt, but absolutely critical in reshaping America.

The media, women's publications, and TV in the forms of talk shows, reality TV shows, and sitcoms have successfully portrayed men in our culture as doddering, thoughtless, hapless clods. These upright dogs with paychecks are but a necessary evil (it takes two members of the *opposite* sex to procreate, after all). In addition to this "need for seed," even radical feminists begrudgingly admit that these Neanderthals do bring income-generating ability and some form of protection to the party, but that's about it. Sadly, many in Christendom do little, if anything, to dispel this notion and, worse, often perpetuate this myth. A cottage industry has emerged, which seeks to accentuate the *differences* between men and women. TV shows and stand-up comics have been illustrating these differences for years in order to get laughs.

Recently, however, several books, seminars, workshops, and retreats have sprung up (many of which are sanctioned by credible ministries) to help men and women in the church understand their differences and hopefully have a better marriage. I think that, in general, most of these things are helpful, and the people running them have good intentions. However, if we're not careful, we set the bar too low for husbands by perpetuating the silly notion that men are simply incapable of doing the dishes, cooking a meal, doing the laundry, helping the kids with homework, remembering anniversaries, etc. etc. Satan's job is far easier, as it pertains to husbands fulfilling Ephesians 5:25, when guys fall back on the "I'm just a guy" defense.

It's funny that men are a little fuzzy when it comes to Ephesians 5:25, yet they can enthusiastically quote Ephesians 5:22 which says, "*Wives submit to your own husbands as you do to the Lord.*" Husbands, it is incumbent upon you to execute Ephesians 5:25, regardless of how unlovable you may find your wife to be at times. As the leader of the home, you can't commit to seriously trying to execute Ephesians 5:25 when and *if* your wife gets with the program and commits to executing Ephesians 5:22. It doesn't work that way. If Jesus Christ had waited for the church to get its act together before He gave His life for us, we would all be destined for Hell!

Guys, you have to commit to this 100% regardless of how difficult it is. You shoot yourself in the foot before you even start if you have the attitude, "Well I'll try, but I just can't do it because

I'm a guy." Trust me, you're better than that. Don't believe Satan's lies. You *can* do all those sensitive guy things and still be a strong leader. You need look no further than the greatest male leader who ever lived, Jesus Christ, as your role model.

Men, think back in your life to all the great leaders you looked up to or worked for. One of the reasons you respected them, took guidance from them, and worked so hard for them was because you knew that they would never ask you to do something they wouldn't do themselves and that they had your back. Now compare and contrast those leaders with other people you worked for who were compassionless bullies who didn't know the first thing about the job they were asking you to do. We've all been in both of those situations. You work your guts out for the first type of leader and you have contempt for the second type.

Husbands, your home is falling apart because you are not *sincerely* trying to do those things that mean so much to your wife. You're waiting for *her* to get it together, and then you'll *try* to address your wife's concerns. Christ guides us, protects us, and blesses us despite our waywardness. Why? Because He loves us immeasurably. You should love your wife the same way. Once you make the commitment to execute Ephesians 5:25, no matter how your wife responds to you, you have started to reshape your marriage. Your wife will start to execute Ephesians 5:22 because she now knows that you are trying to understand her and please her. If you truly demonstrate that you are committed to this, she will follow your lead.

This whole process may take time, but it can and will happen. You will start to reshape your home as your children witness a transformation in Dad which leads to a transformation of both of their parents. The whole thing will start to work as God designed it to. This "new you" will find it easier to build up your children.

(Ephesians 6:4 states: – *Fathers, do not exasperate your children; instead, bring them up in the training and instruction of the Lord.*), and they too will be willing to follow their dad's lead. If this simple commitment on the part of husbands started replicating itself in every home across this great nation, we would really start to reshape America.

WIVES

It's 5:00, and your hectic day is starting to wind down. You're fried from dealing with work, the kids, the house. *You* worked hard today and it's time for *you* to do what *you* wanna do tonight. You imagine "the handoff": that magical moment when your husband walks through the door, and you get a well-deserved reprieve from the craziness. You left your husband a quick voicemail earlier in the day *telling* him what last two ingredients you needed for tonight's dinner, evaporated milk and Swiss cheese. Once he comes through the door you'll turn him toward the family's simmering dinner and instruct him to add those ingredients and finish up the cooking. As dinner simmers, you're going to *tell* him for the twentieth time to fix that hinge on the kitchen cupboard since it finally broke off in your hands today, and *you're* not going to live in this "dump" one more day. Finally, as you saunter out the door for a much-deserved walk in the neighborhood, you tell him to listen to the voicemail from the bill collector who wants to get paid. To add insult to injury, you can't resist one more parting shot: "I wish you made more money!"

Unbeknownst to you, your husband had a rough day as well. Despite telling you for several weeks that today was the big day (the day he learned if he got the promotion or not), you didn't even say a formal goodbye to him this morning, let alone any words of encouragement. Sadly, your middle-aged husband learned that he was beat out, yet again, for a promotion that the family desperately needed. The fact that his latest underqualified opponent is twenty years younger than he is makes it sting even more. While driving home in a daze, he got in a minor car accident which will undoubtedly raise his car insurance premium. Lastly, his mom called and told him that his father was again admitted to the hospital, and this time things look pretty bad.

As your husband stirs dinner and gets out the tool box to fix the cupboard, he wonders how you can be so insensitive. He thinks to himself, "She didn't even ask if I got the promotion." While you clear your mind with a brisk walk, your husband does his best to honor the Lord, meditating on Ephesians 5:25.

This is a train wreck waiting to happen. Fresh off a great walk, you're famished. Your refreshed attitude turns south quickly as you taste dinner—and it's awful. You ask your husband what's up with dinner: "Didn't you add the milk and cheese?" He looks at you like you have three heads, partly because of the day he had and partly because he has no idea what you're talking about.

You see, his day was so bad that he didn't even retrieve your message. Being focused only on *your* crummy day, you start to berate him: "Why can't you even master a simple task like bringing home two grocery items? Are you that worthless?" Despite the fact that the cupboard was finally fixed, you complain that it took months of nagging to get it done. Next, it's time to lambaste him for his anemic earning power. "If you made more money, these bill collectors wouldn't be calling us day and night." This is just what a middle-aged man wants to hear hours after he has once again fallen short at work. He retreats to a remote part of the house wondering why his wife thinks he's such a failure and, worse, starting to believe it himself. She retreats to another part of the house wondering why he can't just get it together and thinking maybe she would have been better off with someone else.

Sound familiar? It does if you're honest. The sad thing is that this didn't have to happen. If the woman had been faithfully meditating on Ephesians 5:22-24 as long as her husband had been meditating on Ephesians 5:25, this fight could have been averted.

Ladies, communicating with your husband is essential for any marriage to work. I know you know this better than your husband does, but please be mindful of what you say and how you say it. Many of the things you say to your husband absolutely need to be said, just not right now. The time you choose to broach heavy issues can make all the difference in the world. Just because you need to talk doesn't mean he should listen. Most of the time he should recognize that you are bursting and need to clear the air. He should graciously accommodate you nine times out of ten. But sometimes, it's just not the time, and you need to be mindful of that.

How you say what needs to be said is also of critical importance. This is not a need that's exclusive to either gender, either. Basic human decency dictates that we treat each other with respect. After all, you are talking to God's son or daughter.

Becky and Ron had been struggling with how and when to discuss "heavy" issues with each other. After many disastrous "discussions," they found themselves retreating to separate areas of the house just to get away. Becky sometimes found it difficult to express herself constructively, so she often found herself writing a letter to Ron which she slipped under his door after every argument.

This drill infuriated Ron, as the letters were basically demeaning manifestos letting him know how bad of a husband he was and that he had better shape up. Over the years the letters became more tempered and constructive and, thankfully, less frequent, as the couple fought less. Ron responded better, but he still found himself harboring resentment and animus toward Becky, regardless of how hard he tried to purge himself of those feelings.

One day, the light bulb in Ron's head went on. It was the perfect storm: a great message by Pastor James McDonald followed by a huge fight culminating in another letter. But this time was different. Pastor McDonald was addressing the men in the congregation and telling them why, despite their best efforts to "shape up," they still failed to love their wives in an Ephesians 5:25 way. He posited the notion that maybe they were not truly repentant for their feelings and their subsequent actions toward their wives. Asking God and your wife for forgiveness to simply get on with life is not how God defines true repentance. Shortly after the message, yet another fight ensued (on Valentine's Day, ouch!), and Becky and Ron's retreating to their usual corners followed.

A note was passed under the door and Ron reflexively thought, "Okay, here we go again." However, this note was different. Although Becky's notes had become progressively more loving and constructive, this one was truly amazing. It was so amazing that at the risk of insulting Becky, Ron told her that he almost thought she didn't write it. Becky replied, "I didn't. God did." Unlike many of her previous letters, which took her some time to write, this one was written in two minutes, all the more amazing since Becky hates to write.

This was truly a God-inspired letter. After empathizing with Becky's feelings of pain and despair, Ron felt truly indicted for causing this anguish; he was broken and *unequivocally* repentant. With her permission, I am sharing with you the note Becky gave Ron that helped him to finally turn the corner in his relationship with her.

MY VALENTINE'S DAY WISH

I want to be loved for who I am, not what I look like. I want to be loved for who I am, not hated for who I used to be. It doesn't seem to matter what I do... you react to what you think *I'm going to do or say. I want to be loved for who I am, not rejected for the things you* think *I'm going to do or say. I want to be loved for who I am and I want you to realize that the things that you don't like about me have helped make you the success that you are today. I'm not a terrible person, even though you make me feel that way. I don't want to start over with someone else, but it seems I don't have a chance at making it work with you—too much has happened between us... too much history that can't be erased. It's easier at this point not to be loved than it is to be hurt by you again. I'll take peace over passion—at least for now. Life is busy and crazy enough to drown out any desires for more than what I have now. But someday the walls I've put up may crumble and I may want more, but you'll be too angry then to ever give more. So I pray that God erases the past and we get a fresh start—no history to cloud today's reality. I pray that God can take the hurt away.*

The husband doesn't have the option of opting out when it comes to his obligation to his wife; the same is true for the wife. Your level of submission to your husband is not in direct proportion to how loveable he is or isn't. As the great Charles Stanley often says, "Obey God and leave the consequences to him."[85] Wives, when God tells you to submit, you should submit. Much of the problem with this concept is rooted in society's negative view of submission. American culture views submission as inferiority, but nothing could be further from the truth. God makes it very clear that men and women are of equal value in his eyes.

Genesis 1:27 says, *"So God created mankind in his own image, in the image of God he created them; male and female he created them."*

We get into trouble before we even start navigating the challenges of marriage when we look at the husband/wife relationship as a 50-50 proposition. More than a few enter into marriage under the false premise that when one party or the other starts to exact more dominance in a given area, that there is an imbalance of power. For example, the wife expresses to her husband that she is really concerned with the amount of time that he spends watching TV. The man perceives this as an affront to his authority, and the balance of power is shifted from 50-50 to 53-47 because she is obviously assuming more of the upper hand in the relationship.

This thinking is whacked and flawed. She is merely bringing something to her husband's attention that needs to be brought to his attention. Remaining silent about something that affects so many facets of the family is not submission; it's stupidity. And thinking your wife should remain silent about it to fulfill her obligation to submit to you is even dumber. Once we realize that the husband/wife dynamic is not a 50-50 proposition but a 100-100 proposition, we can more effectively carry out the roles God has designed for us. Wives, you can never fulfill your role as your husband's greatest ally unless you understand what he needs and how meeting those needs will make him a better husband, father, and citizen.

PARENTS

I fully recognize and appreciate that there are a myriad of parenting situations in society today. The idyllic mom and dad who are blissfully married and parenting in lockstep with their children's best interest in mind doesn't always happen. And even though many parents in less than traditional parenting structures do a fine job of parenting, the cornerstone of effective parenting is to first start with a loving, committed, and married two-parent unit of one man and one woman leading the household. Satan knows very well that the future of any civilization rests on the strength of the family and the foundation of marriage, specifically. It's instructive to read Malachi 2:15 which says, *"Has not the one God made you? You belong to him in body and spirit. And what does the one God seek? Godly offspring. So be on your guard, and do not be unfaithful to the wife of your youth."* God knew that the marriage bond was vitally important and we as a culture should view it as vitally important as well.

Highlighted by, but not starting with, Hillary Clinton's book, *It Takes a Village,* many in our society have been downplaying the importance of parents in the raising of productive citizens. MSN-BC's Melissa Harris-Perry is undoubtedly of this mindset, making comments like, "Kids belong to whole communities."[86] Being a talk show host, I fully recognize how easy it is to take something out of context or to be taken out of context. Many statists' comments are egregious enough that we don't *have* to take them out of context. Furthermore, when we do this, we set ourselves up to be labeled as demagogues and our credibility as ambassadors for Christ is greatly hampered, so I will tread cautiously here.

I believe Ms. Harris-Perry when she asserts that she feels that parents have first and primary responsibility for their children and that the private sphere of our homes and families deserve great deference in policy and practice. However, it's some of her comments on society's role in shaping our kids that I find troubling. Ms. Harris-Perry says, "This is about whether we as a society, expressing our collective will through our public institutions, including our government, have a right to impinge on individual freedoms in order to advance a common good."[87]

Sounds great but...who's defining what "common good" is? Our government (at all levels), our institutions of learning, our media, and sometimes even our churches, can be dominated by a preponderance of godless, left-leaning individuals, whose definition of "common good" can infringe big time on your ability to raise your children in a godly manner. Conversely, if those institutions are populated by individuals who are first and foremost steeped in the word of God, that "common good" might be a whole lot closer to your vision for your child's future.

What does the word of God say about parenting? Proverbs 22:6 says, *"Start children off on the way they should go, and when they are old they will not turn from it."* It seems that everything in our culture is purposely designed to de-program the good values that parents try to instill in their kids. Peers, television, radio, Internet, entertainment industry, many schools, and the law are just some of the many areas that can be minefields for our children.

We hear a lot about peer pressure. Peers are your child's neighbors, classmates, teammates, and general contemporaries in society. The amount of sway any peer has over your kid is directly proportional to how solid of a foundation you have laid for them. Despite your tireless efforts to change society for the better, there will always be bad kids out there. The amount of influence these children have on your son or daughter is, however, largely in your hands.

Your child's friends, on the other hand, are people that you and your child have let into your inner sanctum. Hopefully, your child has taken the task of cultivating friends very seriously. Thoughtful parents and children don't just fall into relationships with other kids. As the ole adage goes: "Show me your friends, and I'll show you your future." How upstanding (or less than upstanding) your child's friends are is an excellent gauge for how swayable your child may be to negative peer pressure. Children who are taught to think highly of themselves and have high standards and criteria for association are far less likely to fall prey to people and forces that will take them off course.

The first thing we can do as parents is instill in our children that they are royalty as children of the most high God. 1 Peter 2:9 says, *"But you are a chosen people, a royal priesthood, a holy nation, God's special possession, that you may declare the praises of him who called you out of darkness into his wonderful light."* Once this has been taught and reaffirmed constantly to your child, we can next move onto teaching our kids how children of the most high God conduct themselves. Too often when raising kids, we incentivize them to behave in a certain way by teaching them that "if you do this, then this will happen."

Even though I firmly believe in the consequences of good or bad behavior, we must be careful with this notion. We want our kids to behave appropriately and associate with like-minded friends because we love Jesus, want to be like Him, and want to obey Him. If this is the child's primary reason for doing what is right, then they won't simply do the right things to get positive results. However, having said that, the child will most likely avoid the pitfalls of life if they do adhere to biblical principles; it's simply a matter of motivation.

Please don't misconstrue anything I've said as a call to make sure your children never associate with certain types of kids. Jesus Christ associated with sinners for the purpose of showing them God's love and His plan for their lives. Jesus Himself tells us in Mark 2:17, *"On hearing this, Jesus said to them, "It is not the healthy who need a doctor, but the sick. I have not come to call the righteous, but sinners."*

If we as parents do our job of instilling biblical principles in our kids at home, we will be far less inclined to keep them in a bubble in order to insulate them from peer pressure. If we do this effectively, it will be less scary for us when our biblically grounded kids "mix it up" with others who might not be so biblically grounded, if they've ever heard the gospel at all. Once you've gotten over the temptation to insulate your children from these kids, it will then be easier for you to get excited as you watch your kids further God's kingdom by sharing the gospel with their peers.

Action Steps

1. Ask God to help you critically assess the shape of your family.

2. Ask yourself: What is my role in making my family better?

3. Ask God to give you the willingness to execute the things necessary to make your family better and then the ability to do those things.

4. Ask yourself: What is the role of the government, my church, and my community in strengthening the family?

10

Ambassadors for Christ

CHILDREN

Whether he knew it or not, Chris's future was *eternally* altered on that fateful day back in 1996 when he met Lauren, a sweet Christian girl who sat next to him in English class.

Chris was headed down a path of destruction, running with a crowd who smoked pot and drank alcohol, and would soon graduate to harder drugs, costing some of them their lives. Chris was awakened by these tragedies and started to realize his mortality.

God often gives us warnings to shape up and seek Him, yet many of us fail to recognize them. Even when we do, we often reflect on their meaning only briefly, then the storm passes and we no longer have time for spiritual things. These are critical times for anyone. Fortunately for Chris, Lauren exploited this opportunity and began to show Chris the love of Christ.

She helped Chris with his studies and was genuinely concerned for him. This was new for Chris. Lauren could have easily stopped there, telling God that she had done her "good deed" for the semester, but this wasn't token, perfunctory witnessing. Lauren was all in. One day she surprised Chris by inviting him to her sweet-sixteen birthday party. Now Chris was really starting to think. It's one thing to help a guy from the wrong side of the tracks with his homework, but to invite him into her inner circle? What's going on here?

At the party, Lauren introduced Chris to Michelle, a youth worker at Lauren's church. Chris didn't understand what a youth worker was; he just knew that Michelle cared for him the same way that Lauren did. I believe they call that the love of Christ. Chris began to pass up parties with his old friends to spend more time with Lauren, Michelle, and the kids from the youth group. Although the message of Jesus wasn't new to Chris, the way they shared it and demonstrated it was. Michelle always let Chris know that she was praying for him. She prayed fervently that Chris would hunger to learn more about Jesus.

Her prayers were answered when Chris started attending Sunday morning church with his new-found friends. This Christianity was very different from the performance-based Christianity that disinterested him in the past. This Christianity was very focused on the sacrifice Jesus Christ endured on Chris's behalf. Chris learned how his sins could not only be forgiven but remembered no more. Unbelievable! What a radical departure from the lack of forgiveness Chris had experienced at the hands of family and friends.

Now was the time. Michelle invited him out for lunch with the hope of leading him to Christ. She wrote Romans 6:23 on a napkin and began to share the gospel with Chris. Paul tells us in this verse; *"For the wages of sin is death, but the gift of God is eternal life in Christ Jesus our Lord."* Chris had heard this message numerous times, but Michelle encouraged him to *believe* it in his heart, make Jesus the Lord of his life, and start walking with Him. On November 7, 1996 Chris became a Christian! Chris knew he was on the right track when a girl at school stopped him in the hall and asked, "Wow, you used to sell drugs and now you want to tell people about Jesus? What's up with that?"

You'll be happy to know that Chris has been all in for Jesus ever since. After graduating from high school, Chris earned a graduate degree in theology, and become a youth pastor at the very same church where it all began. Amazing! Chris is now challenging his students to show the love of Christ by inviting their classmates to youth group. The gospel just keeps marching on. Obviously the Lord wanted Chris to become a child of God, as He does *all* of us. 1 Timothy 2:3-4 says, "*This is good, and pleases God our Savior, who wants all people to be saved and to come to a knowledge of the truth.*" Make no mistake, *He* is the only one who saves. However, in some wondrous way, He chooses us to lead people to Him. With that in mind, I shudder to think of what would have become of Chris had he not gone down a path of righteousness. God bless Lauren, a lowly high school student who stepped out of her comfort zone to heed God's call to reach out to a lost soul.

Chris, Michelle, Lauren, and many of the kids Chris mentors have one thing in common: they're all in for Christ. They're not just "playing" when it comes to their faith. Unfortunately, the majority of Christian kids are not all in. A sobering 75% of them simply abandon their faith when they go to college. According to Pastor John Lawley, "It is well intentioned but sadly ineffectual to simply raise your child in a Godly home and make sure they go to church every Sunday." Maybe in the good old days that was good enough; but today, the number of things pulling your child away from Christ is staggering.

Pastor Lawley asserts that the two biggest factors in a child growing stronger in their faith as they enter young adulthood are "Do they have strong intergenerational relationships with mature believers?" and "Are they actively connecting and serving in the church?" If these questions can be answered in the affirmative, there is a strong likelihood that your child will not fall away from their faith when they leave your home. Conversely, if these two things aren't present in your child's life, they will most likely drift away from spiritual things.

Kids today, more than ever, are distracted beyond comprehension. Satan knows this and will throw everything possible at you and your child in order to derail their walk with Christ. You and your spouse need to go above and beyond when it comes to insuring your kids will stay true to their biblical foundation as they embark upon this thing called life. Making sure that your children cultivate great relationships with other mature believers is one very good step in the right direction. Youth pastors and godly parents simply aren't enough. Your children need other adults they can confide in and learn from in order to flourish. Chris's relationship with Michelle was a good example of this. For obvious reasons, it's often easier for your child to open up to adults other than their parents.

Your child should be connecting and serving in the church. The more connected your child is with other believing kids, the less likely they'll be to withdraw and subsequently fade away when life's challenges become overwhelming. The development of solid Christian relationships will foster accountability, and they'll develop into more committed followers of Christ. This deeper relationship with the Lord and their believing peers will stir a desire to serve in some capacity, and this is a good thing. The kids who look at church or youth group as spectators, who are obliged to attend on Wednesdays or Sundays because their parents make them, have no skin in the game. They are not motivated by a love of Christ to be His ambassador. They become distracted and eventually wooed away by something that seems more exciting or culturally relevant. Christ becomes an afterthought, and is eventually nowhere to be found in their lives.

Pastor Chris was a child who grew up to certainly reshape America, but do the children he now mentors really have a part in reshaping America? I mean, what does the average child know about social ills, oppressive taxation, or social injustice? Well, not much if their parents, teachers, or pastors haven't taught them the first thing about them. However, if you think about it, strong, compassionate, well-adjusted leaders all have to come from somewhere. Who we are today is directly related to how we were raised yesterday. Let's assume that you are doing a pretty good job of raising your child to be a conscientious citizen. Encourage your child to set the bar high in terms of what they are going to do to impact the world!

In my years as a talk radio host, I observed a recurring pattern with listener call-ins. The caller would start some rant about this problem or that, and they would expect me to either validate their complaints or disagree, but we devoted very little time to solving problems. If we're doing our jobs, our children should already be developing problem-solving skills that will equip them to tackle some of the daunting problems this country faces.

What should you encourage your child to be or to do? First, start by asking God what *He* would like your child to be when they grow up. Once He starts speaking to you about it, pray that He starts to impress His desires on your child. Next, ask your child what they would like to do to impact the world for Christ. Often, your kids will be impacted for life by what they heard at a Christian retreat or in a Sunday school message. Start talking to your child early and often about things that pertain to their future. Children who were raised in a godly home will be less likely to succumb to cultural pressure once they start navigating life. Conversely, children raised in a home which is indifferent to God or, worse yet, hostile to biblical principles, will not only succumb to these pressures but will champion them.

Now we have to be even more vigilant because of the legalization of marijuana. As I write this book, six states have legalized the recreational use of marijuana with several others decriminalizing it to the point of ridiculousness. The legalization lobby has creatively positioned their drug as a "mellow" drug. In a dangerous world where violent criminals are often high on chemicals which foster aggression, this is a shrewd move.

Conveniently missing from their marketing campaign is the glaringly obvious fact that marijuana is a HUGE demotivator. I had the misfortune of getting into one of those "should we legalize marijuana" debates the other day. The people with whom I was talking didn't really want to debate; they just wanted to shout me down. One of them went down the "you're a puritan" route while the other was merely young and naïve to the dangers of the drug. They attempted to refute my initial argument that eventually a lack of motivation, laziness, and ambivalence to being productive would eventually ensue after years of regular pot use. Their assertion was that these types of individuals were pretty much destined to be losers regardless, so what's the point of criminalizing pot for the rest of us?

Feeling buoyed, they went on to site numerous successful people who routinely smoke pot yet have risen to lofty heights. Realizing I was losing badly, I tried to have my friends look at pot smokers on a bell curve. I asserted that the lazy and unmotivated as well as the highly motivated, bright, and talented were in the minority and were outliers on opposite sides of the curve. The reality is that the majority of society makes up the lion's share of the curve. If this is even remotely accurate, there are a whole lot of people who could go either way as far as a bright future is concerned. These individuals don't need too much to knock them off course.

I contend that these people will not achieve the goals God has planned for them if they are compromised by a drug like marijuana. The danger of this drug is its insidious nature. You simply can't go to work or school drunk or on heroin, but you can function (for a time) high on marijuana. The disinterest in being the best you can be develops slowly among routine pot smokers. We will start to realize the long-term physiological and psychological effects of marijuana as the drug becomes more socially acceptable.

The frightening thing is that there are *children as young as ten* who are getting the message that the use and even the distribution of marijuana is okay. School officials in Greeley, Colorado were recently alerted to the fact that a ten-year-old boy was selling the drug to other classmates. Another student was attempting to trade his edible marijuana for a smokeable form of the drug.[88] What is this world coming to?! We traded bologna for peanut butter and jelly in my elementary school. Sadly, the children involved were not expelled or suspended, as administrators felt it was more important to focus on the parents, urging them to take better care of their newly legal recreational marijuana. This is madness. Did officials in the State of Colorado not anticipate this coming? Gina Carbone, who helped found the group Smart Colorado, which publicizes concerns about legalization's impact on children, said it best: "Pot is celebrated, glorified and promoted. Kids are watching adults, and this is the way adults are behaving."[89] Sadly, I fear that this is just the tip of the iceberg.

Lastly, we must take a stand for our children. Cultural decay is everywhere. It's growing at an alarming rate, and fewer and fewer adults who know right from wrong are standing up for our children's future. I fully understand and appreciate the fact that standing up for what is right sometimes feels like you're fighting locusts with a tennis racket. Regardless, God expects us to stand up for good vs. evil even when it's uncomfortable. Whether these culture wars are won or lost is irrelevant in terms of our obedience and obligation to do the right thing. God is pleased when we stand up against things that harm our children.

I recently boarded a very crowded plane for a cross-continental flight. The only seat left was between a young dad who was holding his young toddler in his lap for five hours (kudos to you, Dad), and a middle-aged man who was watching a movie on his iPad. As the flight progressed, I found myself glancing over at the man's movie from time to time and was shocked to discover that what he was watching was very inappropriate for children, and even sensible adults. It was one of those "should I get involved?" moments.

Heretofore, adults routinely made things their business if someone in public was doing something that was just not right; not so today. The results of such interventions can end very badly. However, since obedience is at the cornerstone of everything in this book and we are called to reshape our country for the better, I decided to say a quick prayer to the Lord: "Lord, if you want me to intervene, make it clear to me that this movie is as inappropriate as I suspect it is." Shortly after this prayer, a *very* inappropriate scene unfolded, and I had had enough.

I tapped the gentlemen on the shoulder and told him that he shouldn't be watching this type of movie in such close proximity to the child on my right. His response was interesting. I wouldn't have been so taken aback if he had laughed out loud, called me a puritan, or simply told me to mind my own business. He sheepishly snickered and said, "The kid's not even watching it." So just because this small boy had not yet seen what I had seen, should we wait until he does?

The fact that this man was oblivious to the potential collateral damage of this filth was sobering. The child may not have been watching but God is. Although the man turned his iPad a few degrees to his left to placate me, he kept watching the movie. As indifferent to right and wrong as he appeared to be, there was obviously a chink in his armor. Quite frankly, he didn't have to turn the screen at all. Furthermore, I believe God was working on him as throughout the course of the movie, probably as things got racier and racier, I watched him turn his iPad further to the left, and sometimes he even draped his forearms and hands over the screen. He got the message. A small victory, no doubt, but every long journey starts with a simple step. I was proud of myself, not because I changed the world, but because I obeyed God's very simple request and *He* changes the world one step at a time.

TEACHERS

As all of you teachers know, many students arrive at school ill-prepared. It would be bad enough if I was referring to their lack of preparation for their course work, but it goes much deeper than that. Not having their math homework done is the least of their worries. Many of these kids come from homes where both parents are working way too many hours and are far too distracted with their own selfish desires to even think about raising their children up to be productive, conscientious citizens. Other students come from single-parent homes where the challenge of being a kid without the benefit of having a mom and dad living in the same home and working together for their good is heartbreaking. Still other students are being raised by extended family members or in foster care situations. Lastly, more and more students are coming from homes (and I use that term loosely) where absolutely no one cares. It's only by the grace of God that these kids are even going to school. If they are lucky enough to make it to your classroom, they sometimes show up with things other than school supplies.

Take, for example, the first-grade student at John Barry Elementary School in Philadelphia who arrived at school with eleven bags of heroin, resulting in twenty students being hospitalized.[90] This unfortunate urchin has little choice but to grow up in a "home" that undoubtedly has no regard for anything that is conducive to preparing a youngster for life. A student facing any and sometimes all of these challenges is going to require extra work on the teacher's part. A room full of these students presents a dilemma that no teacher should ever have to face.

All of the aforementioned scenarios and many more can very easily lead to a situation where a child is simply drifting through life without the proper guidance to become a productive citizen. This is where you come in. Imparting knowledge to students within your particular subject-matter area is only part of the equation. Think back to the most memorable teachers you had. They may not have been the best, but you remember them just the same. You remember them because they impacted you. A great teacher is perceptive enough to realize that their role in a child's development goes far beyond the subject that they teach. The most impactful teachers teach us about life.

My daughter's eighth-grade math teacher was a former businessman who decided to pursue public school teaching late in life. Much of the wisdom he imparted to his students had very little to do with math and much more to do with the valuable life lessons he had learned.

At the beginning of each school year, my wife and I scheduled meetings with my children's teachers far in advance of any meetings mandated by the school district. We did this to convey our expectations and to basically "size up" the teacher. Interestingly enough, the teachers' educational pedigree, subject-matter expertise, or even competence were not the primary things we were investigating. What we wanted to know was, do these teachers *really* care about the kids they teach? I'll take a teacher who is willing to work long hours because they care over a teacher who is otherwise more qualified. Caring teachers look beyond their lesson plans and their student's ability to meet those objectives. They don't want to see one child slip through the cracks. They take an interest when their students fall behind and don't just go through the motions in order to help them. Caring teachers take an interest in what's going on with the student's home life and pick up on how their students interact with their peers.

Sometimes these teachers have a kid whom no one else really cares about. Instead of just feeling sad, they step in and become that student's reason to succeed. They fill the voids that seem to be in every aspect of the child's life. They realize if they don't fill those voids; nobody will. A teacher can literally be the last line of defense before a kid drifts off into an irretrievable abyss of hopelessness.

Imparting words of wisdom and guiding our children in a godly manner has become increasingly challenging as teachers (who are essentially supposed to be agents of the state), are not supposed to invoke the name of God or otherwise guide students in a religious manner. As previously noted, the separation of church and state was never mentioned in our Constitution; nevertheless, administrators and teachers have become so hyperphobic to mixing the two that religious liberties get trampled on almost daily in an attempt to not offend anyone.

In order to do their part in reshaping America, teachers need to become intimately familiar with what their rights are when it pertains to their religious liberties and the religious liberties of their students. Most teachers are woefully ignorant about what they can and cannot do in an educational setting, an ignorance that often leads them to err on the side of not saying or doing anything that, in an effort to play it safe, could be perceived as religious.

When my daughter was in third grade, her teacher asked the students to make a star for the "holiday tree." The star was to be blank on both sides so the students could write their wishes for the holiday season. My daughter wrote on one side of her holiday star that she wished every child would have a present for Christmas. On the other side she wrote that she wished everyone would know Jesus. Once the task was completed, the children put their stars on the "holiday tree." When the teacher saw what my child had written on her star, she told her it would have to be turned over to the other side, so she wouldn't offend anyone. My child was sad and confused. Unfortunately, her teacher was confused as well. Allowing my child to express herself in the manner she chose was in no way, shape, or form endorsement by the teacher or the school of a particular religion. The sad thing about this occurrence was that the teacher was not some militant, anti-Christian zealot; she was merely ignorant.

A similar incident happened in Temecula, California, where first-grader Bryn Williams was silenced by her teacher when she attempted to fulfill the requirements of an assignment to share a family *Christmas* tradition with the class. Bryn brought in the Star of Bethlehem and was in the middle of explaining to the class what it meant to her and her family at Christmas time when her teacher shouted, "Stop right there! Go take your seat!" The teacher explained to Bryn, in front of her classmates, that she was not allowed to talk about the Bible or share its verses.

Advocates for Faith and Freedom, a non-profit legal firm whose stated mission is to "protect religious liberty in the courts," stated that the First Amendment's Establishment Clause "prohibits disapproval and hostility toward religion," and that while teachers and public officials should refrain from establishing or endorsing religion, there is no legal prohibition against students doing so. The absurdity of this incident is that Bryn didn't even do that. She simply brought in a prop which helped her convey to her fellow classmates her family's Christmas tradition. Temecula Valley Unified School District currently has a policy in place that states "Students may express their beliefs about religion in their homework, artwork and other class work if the expression is germane to the assignment." To tell a kid to shut up and sit down when she brings in the *Star of Bethlehem* to explain a family *Christmas* tradition is madness! If you are bright or dim, religious or atheist, you can't possibly have a hard time understanding that the Star of Bethlehem *is* germane to the Christmas story.[91]

When an F5 tornado struck Moore, Oklahoma in 2013, Rhonda Crosswhite, a brave sixth-grade teacher at Plaza Tower Elementary School, found herself sheltering in a bathroom stall with six frightened children. "I did the teacher thing that we're probably not supposed to do," she later recalled. "I prayed and I prayed out loud." As the violence raged and her students cried out to her for protection, Rhonda openly appealed to the Lord, saying, "God, please don't take these kids today."[92] The fact that this brave teacher, in the wake of comforting her students, felt ashamed for calling on her Lord in a life-or-death situation illustrates where we are as a society. She's lucky she lives in Oklahoma. In the Northeast, this admission may have cost her her job.

WORKPLACE

Bob approaches the building he has driven to countless times in the last ten years. His stomach churns once again with the anxious anticipation of another tumultuous day. You see, Bob started with this company ten years ago as a celebrated junior executive filled with talent, enthusiasm, and the hope of climbing the corporate ladder, a noble dream shared by thousands of young men. Ten years later, these hopes are all but gone. He suffers from the all the realities of middle-age: he's gained a few pounds, lost some hair, and doesn't have that cut-throat drive that the younger alpha males have.

These inevitable realities are compounded by the fact that he is the only believer in an office of 25 people. His ethical compass seems to be a liability, as he has been passed over numerous times by other men who have no problem doing whatever it takes to get ahead. His biblical principles have hindered his ability to play the game of office politics, which has further lessened his chance of career advancement. Oh, I forgot to mention that his new boss is a flaming jerk who is fifteen years his junior…OUCH! Bob is not unlike many men in the workforce: overqualified, underpaid, and thoroughly frustrated.

Sound familiar? Sure it does, because it's probably you, someone you know, or even someone you live with. Bob is starting to say to God, "Where are you? Can't you see that I'm getting a raw deal here? I'm outta here!" Everything in this world is telling Bob to move on but God might be telling him to stay. In fact, He probably is. If you and I bolted every time our job became unpalatable, we would miss some of the most wonderful life lessons God wants to teach us.

Being the best employee you can be will reshape America. Just think of how much more productive this country would be if every employee did their best, every day. James 1:2-4 says: "*Consider it pure joy, my brothers, whenever you face trials of many kinds, because you know that the testing of your faith produces perseverance. Let perseverance finish its work so that you may be mature and complete, not lacking anything.*" It doesn't matter how much of a jerk your boss is, how little you are getting paid, or how much you hate your job. You must do your job as unto the Lord for as long as you are blessed to have one. Perseverance at a job where conditions are difficult builds character. Maybe God has you in this job for a reason.

We can't just bail every time the going gets tough, but that's exactly what a lot of young people do. If they don't bail, they whine, snipe, gossip, cut corners, and essentially mail it in until they do bail or get fired. This is not God's plan. As bad as some work environments may be, there's always a few people who will notice the fact that you seem to be above the dysfunctional office fray. What a witness for Christ it is to persevere in a Christlike manner when you're being treated unfairly or when you're being taken advantage of! People will be intrigued by how you handle adversity; then you can open up the discussion about what or, specifically, *who* helps you cope with a bad situation.

Bucking up in a bad work environment is not the only way to share the gospel. Many work environments are fantastic. Countless business owners and managers have tried to create an environment where people actually like coming to work. In these settings, turnover is usually low, and the team has been together for a long time. This is a perfect setting to share the gospel. But be warned; once you decide to do this, Satan will start whispering lies in your ear. He'll say, "Are you nuts? Have you looked at the unemployment rate lately? You've got a good thing here; don't go screwing it up with that religious stuff! You're in good standing now, but if you bring up that crap, they're gonna think you're weird."

The lies go on and on until the majority of Christians opt to play it safe and not make waves. These are the folks that "Bible Answer Man" Hank Hanegraff refers to as "undercover Christians." They have their church life over here and their work and social lives over there. This is sad. If you really want to reshape America, you have to realize something: your Christian walk is 24/7, 365 days a year. God doesn't put you in *any* situation accidentally, and where you work is no exception. Having a daily Scripture calendar on your desk, or simply praying silently over your lunch in the break room, are simple ways to start the conversation.

You know as well as I do that there are plenty of times throughout the day that you and your co-workers talk about things that are not work related. Use these times to slowly but surely start witnessing to your colleagues. Giving a co-worker an uplifting tract, inviting them to church, or simply letting them know that you'll be praying for them can be a little out of your comfort zone, but it's very doable. Ask God to help you with this because you're scared. Ask him to bless your willingness to obey Him. You'll find that He will bless your obedience in more than a few ways, and you will start to become very comfortable reaching out to your co-workers. In fact, they might start seeking you out.

One final note on witnessing at the workplace: remember why you are witnessing in the first place: to lead people to a knowing relationship with Christ. This seems to be obvious; however, some peoples' workplace witnessing leaves a lot to be desired. First and foremost, you are at work to work. As much as we are charged to evangelize, we cannot throw common sense out the window.

Christ never wants us to be sanctimonious, contentious, or disruptive at work. Satan loves to use overzealous individuals to *repel* people from the gospel, and we should always be mindful of that. We can very easily respect authority and the workplace mores that those in authority have established *and* effectively witness to our co-workers.

Just because you can't take it anymore and you think it's time to change jobs doesn't mean that it's time to quit. When it's time to move on we'll get the green light from God. Your decision to change jobs must always be filtered through His lens. James 1:5 says, *"If any of you lacks wisdom he should ask God, who gives generously to all without finding fault and it will be given to him."* We need to seek this wisdom, wait until we receive it, and then proceed accordingly in order to be in the vocation God wants us to be in. I have heard a thousand stories about people who have gone from the frying pan to the fire because they were tired of waiting for God to fix their work situation. In these instances, Satan effectively uses the emotions of anger and fear to quickly derail us from the vocational path God has in store for us.

Many of us think that our company, our boss, and the tasks we have to perform are the reasons we are so miserable each day we go to work. However, all of the aforementioned things may not be the problem; you may simply be mismatched or bored with what you are doing. I am well aware of the fact that we all have to pay the bills. However, in the long run, staying in a job where you are simply going through the motions doesn't really make a lot of sense if we want to reshape ourselves, our families, and America. Much of the problem in our country today is due to the fact that very few people really care about anything. When it comes to our vocation, we must strike that delicate balance between knowing when to steadfastly wait on the Lord and stay at a particular job and boldly moving on to the next exciting mission that He has planned for us.

THE GREAT COMMISSION

A return to God and His principles is absolutely vital in order to return to the greatness that God has bestowed upon us. This cannot be achieved without winning souls to Christ. Our country thrives when believers and non-believers alike live by and espouse biblical principles.

It is infinitely easier to do something difficult when you thoroughly understand *why* you do it. Believers understand who our creator is and why Jesus died on the cross. Believers are motivated by being Christlike and pleasing God, rather than just by a love of country. We need more Christians to take the lead in carrying out this mission of reshaping America. When the United States is the third largest mission field in the world, we have a huge problem. That's why the Great Commission is so important. What is the Great Commission? Matthew 28:18-20 says: *"Then Jesus came to them and said, 'All authority in heaven and earth has been given to me. Therefore go and make disciples of all nations, baptizing them in the name of the Father and of the Son and of the Holy Spirit, and teaching them to obey everything I have commanded you. And surely I am with you always, to the very end of the age.'"*

Before you think that *"all the nations"* has little to do with reshaping *our* nation, think again. In the past, few would have disagreed that America was a nation founded on Judeo-Christian principles. People representing a wide variety of nations not only came to this country to be "Americans" but they also fully understood that the essence of being an American was deeply rooted in Judeo-Christian principles. America is not called the melting pot for nothing. Most nations of the world are represented in some fashion in every walk of American life. However, even though the country is actually more diverse today than it has ever been, the desire to assimilate into a distinctly American culture is hardly evident.

This presents a unique opportunity to make disciples of all nations without ever leaving our shores. John Eliot, known as "Apostle to the Indians," was a good example of this. A Puritan missionary, Eliot learned the Algonquian language so he could teach Christian truths to Native American Indians in their own tongue, making disciples of his fellow man.

Of all the things we can do to reshape America, executing the Great Commission is at the top of the list. Jesus charges *all* of us to do this whether we feel like it or not. Furthermore, asserting that "witnessing is just not my thing" doesn't cut it with God because He wants all people to be saved and come to a knowledge of the truth. His desire to see *everyone* come to a relationship with His son Jesus Christ is steeped in His profound love for all of us.

Hell is a very real place. The existence of hell is dismissed, downplayed, and trivialized by many in our culture who simply don't know what they're talking about. I wanted to take the time to cite Saul Alinsky, who has long since passed. The reason I feel the need to do this is twofold: first, this man has unfortunately influenced more than a few of our modern day politicians with his radical beliefs; second, and most importantly, I think it's very important to understand that many in our culture have views on hell that are very similar to Mr. Alinsky's. The following were Mr. Alinsky's thoughts on hell while being interviewed by Playboy magazine:

Alinsky: …if there is an afterlife, and I have anything to say about it, I will unreservedly choose to go to hell.

Playboy: Why?

Alinsky: Hell would be heaven for me. All my life I have been with the have-nots. Over here, if you're a have-not, you're short of dough. If you're a have-not in hell, you're short of virtue. Once I get in to hell, I'll start organizing the have-nots over there.

Playboy: Why them?

Alinsky: They're my kind of people.[93]

Jesus alluding to hell in Matthew 13:42 said, "They will throw them into the blazing furnace, where there will be weeping and gnashing of teeth." We should take hell very seriously and do everything we can to educate people to the dangers of dying without Jesus Christ. Sadly, a few short weeks after Mr. Alinsky made these flippant remarks, he died of a massive heart attack on a street corner in Carmel, California, at age 63.

If our motivation to witness is born out of obligation rather than a genuine love of our fellow man, we will witness in a perfunctory manner, if we even witness at all. In much the same way, our intense love of country and our fellow countrymen should be enough motivation to fervently adopt some of the principles outlined in this book. If we start with love, the daunting task of becoming the best citizens we can be, and urging others to do the same, will be just that: a "labor of love" rather than a hopeless exercise in futility.

Love trumps everything. Love covers a multitude of sins. Don't misunderstand, having a deep-seated hatred of wrong is a good thing and comes from God above. We don't inherently possess this. This truth is in short supply in our culture today. Ambivalence toward sin has paved the way for the incremental decay of everything that is decent in our land; however, one must be very careful to be motivated by a love of God, country, and our fellow man *first* and a hatred of sin *second* when we embark on changing our country for the better.

Ravi Zacharias often quotes an old Indian saying that says, "Once you've cut off a person's nose, there's no point giving him a rose to smell."[94] If one's motivation in changing the world for the better is hatred of sin *first* and love of God, country, and our fellow countryman *second,* we leave ourselves ripe for Satan to shape us into sanctimonious, puritanical caricatures, spewing fire and brimstone in every direction. When this occurs, we actually can become tools for the people/forces that are hell-bent on destroying this country.

Way back when ObamaCare was just a proposal, many rallies sprang up across the nation. The proposed takeover of 1/6 of our economy (health care) to radically change our country in several different was disturbing to a lot of people. These rallies drew attention to many things the Obama Administration was doing or proposing to do that seemed extra-constitutional and overly intrusive. Although the beliefs of the rally goers were steeped in passion, the rallies themselves were, in very large part, peaceful and civil in nature. Rather than focus on the aforementioned generalities, the media (which is often sympathetic to detrimental ideologies) decided to find someone in the crowd that *they* thought would be an "accurate" depiction of who these patriots *really* are. Sure enough, they hit pay dirt.

They found a lunatic in the crowd with a large sign that said *Bury Healthcare With Ted Kennedy.* Senator Kennedy, a decidedly left-leaning politician, had recently succumbed to cancer. Now I ask you, what was paramount in this guy's ideology? Love of God, country, and countrymen, or hatred of what he perceived as sin (the myriad of ills which ObamaCare would spawn)? Let's say for the sake of argument that ObamaCare (then in its fetal stages) was destined to be the downfall of our nation, a notion that is being realized more and more with every passing day. This man's point is totally obscured by his horribly hateful and insensitive shot at a deceased man with whom he happened to disagree. Furthermore, because of the power of the media and the American public's general lack of discernment when it comes to their sources of information, this guy is now the poster boy for the mean-spirited, Tea Party-loving, Neanderthals on the Christian right.

It doesn't matter if he is an aberration; perception is reality. If sane, thoughtful, faith-based citizens aren't extremely careful, we can leave ourselves open to being misquoted, misunderstood and ultimately mischaracterized. Once this occurs, it becomes very easy for our opponents in this culture war to label us, put us in a box, and dispatch us and our principles as "extreme." Once this is effectively done, the apathetic, ignorant, and even the reasonable, turn a deaf ear to what we have to say. The result: we as a nation will continue to, as Judge Robert Bork put it, "slouch toward Gomorrah."

There are many reasons/excuses that we use to avoid taking the Great Commission seriously. Here are just a few:

"Jesus Wasn't Talking to Me; I'm Not a Disciple."

Let's define disciple. *Vine's Expository Dictionary of New Testament Words* defines *disciple* as "A follower or student of a teacher, leader, or philosopher."[95] In the ancient world, the word is most often associated with people who were devoted followers of a great religious teacher. *American Heritage Dictionary* defines *disciple* as, "One who embraces and assists in spreading the teachings of another; a member of the disciples of Christ."

We may not have the robes and the beards (well, some of us might), but I think it's pretty clear that He is talking to us. The more disciples we make, who in turn make more disciples themselves, the faster this country will start moving in the right direction. Numbers matter when it comes to movements. The level of peace and prosperity a country enjoys has always been in direct proportion to the extent with which that culture respects the tenets of God and, more importantly, the God from who those tenets originated.

"Isn't that the Pastor's, Elder's, or Deacon's Job?"

It most certainly is. However, these great men of Christ cannot do this alone, and we cannot expect them to do all the spiritual heavy lifting when it comes to the Great Commission. Unfortunately, many parishioners view church as a spectator sport. God help the pastor if he's not "entertaining" on Sunday. It's not just what you are getting out of it, but also what you are putting into it ("it" being the whole church experience) that is of importance as well.

The good news your pastor is feeding you is not only for your consumption. Biblical worship, education, and brotherly love aren't just for Sunday. God doesn't want you to take the things you learned on Sunday and put them under your hat. You are to live and breathe what you learned on Sunday throughout the week, as a lost world is in need of what you have, whether they know it or not.

"I'm too Busy."

We have *all* used this one to get out of a wide array of obligations in our lives. However, this excuse doesn't cut it with God.

We *all* accomplish what we *want* to do in a given day, and we never seem to get around to doing the things that we really *don't* want to do. If making disciples of men is not a priority for us, it won't get done. Furthermore, busy people tend to come in contact with many others on any given day, so actually they have even more witnessing opportunities.

"I'm Not Outgoing or Gregarious."

Don't worry about it; God can still use you to win souls to Christ. Often times it takes years for someone to come to the Lord, and there are usually several twists and turns in this journey. Just because you're not boldly witnessing to strangers or leading someone in the sinner's prayer does not mean that you can't be an integral part of the process. You never know what part God wants you to play in a person's salvation. We all have talents that He can use to further His kingdom.

One of the more sobering but true reasons that we don't witness is the simple fact that we *just don't want to rub elbows with certain types of people.* Mark 2:17 says: "*On hearing this, Jesus said to them, 'It is not the healthy who need a doctor but the sick. I have not come to call the righteous, but sinners.'*" There are a lot of spiritually sick people in our country today. A society will not last very long without a moral compass. Governmental edicts, fear of law enforcement, or even directives from well-meaning people in our inner sanctums will only sustain a culture for so long. A true desire to "do good" only comes from above. Many of the people in our country who might be characterized as misfits of one form or another are precisely the type of people Jesus wants us to disciple.

"The Whole Witnessing Thing is Just too Weird."

My high school French teacher used to illustrate various cultural differences between Americans and the French. Some of their customs were, to us, pretty weird. When we would say, "That's weird!" he would correct us and say, "It's not weird, it's just different." Admittedly, witnessing to our fellow man in a very fallen world is indeed "different." Witnessing is sadly unusual and out of the ordinary in today's world.

Let's change that and make sharing something wonderful with our brothers and sisters the natural thing to do! Despite knowing the good news of God's love for us, many are embarrassed to even start the process. I'd like to remind these folks what Jesus said in Luke 9:26: *"Whoever is ashamed of me and my words, the Son of Man will be ashamed of them when he comes in his glory and in the glory of the Father and of the holy angels.'"* It's much better to do something that may not be entirely comfortable at first than to just let an opportunity to save someone's life for Christ slip by.

Action Steps

1. Ask yourself: What am I doing to forward the gospel?

2. Ask yourself: What am I doing to encourage and equip others to forward the gospel?

3. Ask God for the willingness and ability to carry out the Great Commission.

11

We Can Do This!

When Israel was oppressed and starving at the hands of the Midianites, God summoned Gideon to raise an army to throw off the yoke of the invader. 32,000 men answered the call, more than enough to vanquish the enemy's 15,000-strong army, but God told Gideon to reduce his force by allowing anyone who trembled with fear at the coming battle to turn back and go home. Gideon lost 22,000 men and instantly went from having a commanding numerical advantage to being seriously outnumbered.

Still God said that Israel's force was too large and commanded Gideon to pare his army yet again until he had only 300 troops. Gideon was now hopelessly outnumbered yet Israel won the war. The secret of their success? *God was with them.* With God's help, a tiny Israelite force of 300 men defeated a mighty army of 15,000.

Great things can be achieved with small numbers if those who are called are willing to put God first and obey him unconditionally. The good news is that although it may appear as if God-fearing, patriotic citizens are in the minority, this is not the case. We are not in any way outnumbered by those who want to tear us down. However, when we're asked to roll up our sleeves and actually *do* something in this cultural fight, the numbers drop off precipitously. This is sad, but perhaps this book will ignite a spark in some of them to get off the sidelines and get into the game. James, the brother of Jesus, tells us in James 4:17, *"If anyone, then, knows the good they ought to do and doesn't do it, it is sin for them."*

Even though you're reading a book about reshaping America, remember that reshaping America is secondary to winning souls for Jesus. This country cannot get back on track without mass revival, and for mass revival to occur we need ambassadors for Christ willing to share the good news of the gospel.

The premise is simple: the more godly folks you have, the more folks you have engaging in godly behavior. These people will become more acutely aware of the sin around them and be offended by it. They will band together and change their local communities for the better. These communities will be role models for other communities and their counties will change for the better. These counties will become role models for entire regions and these regions will become role models for the state. States that are faltering will quickly look to states that are thriving and employ the strategies that turned them around. Hopefully, the country as a whole will get the message that by blessing God, God will bless America. Psalm 33:12 says, *"Blessed is the nation whose God is the Lord, the people he chose for his inheritance."*

Personally, I feel obliged to do more than just go to church and live a Godly life. Don't get me wrong, doing those things would be a great start for more than a few "Christians." However, Christianity is a full time job, and it's a full time job to be a good citizen. So it must require a fair amount of our time if we want to be both. *Anything* worth fighting for requires time and effort. Sadly, I think there are a lot of fully capable, decent folks in this country who would like a better nation but aren't willing to get their hands dirty.

The other day I was assaulted for the thousandth time by some weight-loss commercial touting a drug/pill/diet that will help you "shed pounds *without* changing your lifestyle!" As sad and illogical as this is, droves of people fall for this "have your cake and eat it too" approach to tackling difficult problems. Ask anyone who has battled the bulge and won, for good, (which can take several *years*) and they will tell you that losing weight and *keeping it off for good* requires a lot of hard work on a whole host of fronts. Similarly, the battle to reshape America requires time and effort. Sadly, we've all seen folks who have said the sinner's prayer only to follow up with a life of fruitlessness. Good works will not help you attain salvation, but they are a manifestation of someone who is truly saved.

If we love God, we want to please Him and obediently serve Him, regardless of the time and effort it may require. Similarly, if we love America, it is only logical that we would do whatever it takes to make her better. This is pretty basic stuff that I have personally seen work time and time again; however, despite examples of this "bless God" concept working, a lot of people are simply sitting on their hands while Rome burns. There are many things *everyone* could be doing to right this ship, but, for one reason or another, they aren't doing them.

Sadly, in addition to Christians who have simply chosen not to pay attention to the declining world around them, there are a number who are well aware that the world is going to hell in a handbasket and aren't overly bothered by it. They put up a quasi-fight against what they see as wrong in the culture, but many just go through the motions. These are decent folks who aren't happy with the state of our country, but they read the signs of the times as a validation that Jesus is coming soon. May I remind these folks of Jesus's words in Matthew 24:36: "*But about that day or hour no one knows, not even the angels in heaven, nor the Son but only the Father.*" I'm all for Jesus coming yesterday, but this fatalistic "there's nothing we can do about the inevitability of history" mentality is problematic.

The Apostle Paul admonished the Thessalonians for doing much the same thing. Once Paul declared that the Lord could come at any moment, many Thessalonian believers simply kicked back and waited for it to happen. Paul implored the Thessalonians to "*never tire of doing what is right.*" Many felt that Jesus's return was right around the corner, so they simply shut down and put their lives on autopilot. Paul tells Christians in Romans 12:11 to "*Never be lacking in zeal, but keep your spiritual fervor, serving the Lord.*"

I agree with Kirk Cameron's thoughts in the movie *Monumental*, as he speaks to this phenomenon very well. Mr. Cameron starts the movie with the following preamble:

> I have friends in church that tell me that the worse things get, the better it really is because it means that the end is near and that Jesus is returning. Don't worry that the world is going to hell in a handbasket…just get out of the handbasket. It's part of the plan, it's meant to be, that the whole thing is gonna burn. Really? Because I have kids in this world, I have friends who have children in this world and I want a great future for them, are we supposed to just let it go?![96]

Cameron accurately goes on to say, "We've forgotten what made this nation so successful, healthy, prosperous, and secure in the first place…Maybe if we could go back and talk to the men and women who built this country, they would tell us what we were doing wrong and how to fix it." Mr. Cameron chronicles the fact that our forefathers could easily have thought they were in the end times as well. He points out that the culture was terrible, the nation was bankrupt, the king had tripled the debt, people were slaves, and all were subject to a king who set himself up as God on earth! I'd be looking for Jesus to return myself if I lived in those times!

Mr. Cameron finishes by saying:

> If anyone knew what it was like to live in difficult times, where it looked like the end was near, it was them. But what was their attitude? It wasn't put your head down and get ready for the end of the world. It was "We're getting off the defense and getting on the offense and we see victory in the future." They had a 500-year plan and they went and built a new nation![97]

God loves this country and he didn't bless us wildly for hundreds of years just to watch us destroy it in a few short decades. There is work to be done and God expects us to carry out that work regardless of when He returns.

There's no question that this will be a daunting task. The forces against this country making a comeback are determined. Ephesians 6:12 tells us: *"For our struggle is not against flesh and blood, but against the rulers, against the authorities, against the powers of this dark world and against the spiritual forces of evil in the heavenly realms."* The people who are bent on destroying us are driven—whether they realize it or not—by these forces. Make no mistake, Satan wants America to collapse, and we are well on our way.

Years ago, I wore myself out trying to "save the world." Between work, family, being a good citizen, and my obligations to the church, I was tired. Each night I went to bed exhausted and frustrated, asking myself, "Am I really making a difference?" We don't have to feel this way. If we don't want to feel like we're pushing spaghetti up a hill, we have to take Jesus's advice in Matthew 11:29-30: " *'Take my yoke upon you and learn from me, for I am gentle and humble in heart, and you will find rest for your souls. For my yoke is easy and my burden is light.'* "

Every journey begins with a single step and it's a step we have to take, but be warned: Satan will fill you with discouragement almost before you start. When you talk to an intelligent, decent co-worker and he doesn't even know who his congressman is, you'll be discouraged. When you find out a sister in Christ is not only voting for, but campaigning for, a pro-abortion and pro-gay-marriage candidate, you'll be discouraged. When you try to have a discussion with an elder at your church about some important current event and he looks back at you with glazed eyes, not understanding anything you're saying, you'll be discouraged. When you read statistics that 75% of God-fearing, hardworking, tax-paying believers don't even vote, you'll be discouraged.

Our mission to reshape America should be approached the same way we share the gospel: with one-on-one relationships. This battle will be won at the grassroots level, not through government mandates, but through water-cooler conversations, backyard barbecues, and friendly discussions at your kid's soccer game.

Whatever *your* calling is, be purposeful in the execution of what God wants you to do. A calling from God is great, but his purpose for you will never be fully realized unless you have an action plan. First, ask the Lord what He would like you to do. James 1:5 says, " *If any of you lacks wisdom, you should ask God, who gives generously to all without finding fault, and it will be given to you.*" Meditating on this verse is extraordinarily helpful; however before you read James 1:5, you should claim James 4:7-8 which says: "*Submit yourselves, then to God. Resist the devil, and he will flee from you. Come near to God and he will come near to you. Wash your hands, you sinners, and purify your hearts you double minded.*"

Rest assured, Satan hates this country and doesn't want you or anyone else changing it for the better. He will do his best to block you from fully comprehending what God is telling you through James 1:5. Asking God for wisdom is the first step, but we cannot receive marching orders unless we listen. Listening requires our undivided attention. The ability to pay attention and focus on a wide array of things, let alone something as important as God speaking, has been greatly diminished by the host of distractions you and I face on a daily basis. Satan will exploit these distractions to further his kingdom.

When I first started doing talk radio, it was a much lower-tech world. Listeners couldn't tune in on laptops, iPods, or mobile phones. Talk shows generally couldn't be downloaded to listen to later. You had to be within close proximity of a radio station to hear its signal. The smaller the station, the smaller the signal. When I first started in radio, I was on a 1,000-watt station. This was basically the equivalent of two tin cans connected by a piece of phlegm-coated string. Gross, but accurate.

I had many friends throughout Eastern Pennsylvania who, when they knew I was on the radio, wanted to tune in. Where they were located (proximity) and how many things (obstructions) that were between them and the signal, dictated how well they could *receive* that signal. The impediments that could inhibit the signal could be mountains, valleys, time of day, weather patterns, or equipment malfunction. Distance from God, coupled with countless obstructions (work, material things, frivolous leisure-time activities, associating with the wrong people), could hamper our ability to receive God's signal. When we rid ourselves of these obstructions, we pave the way to more clearly hear what God tells us in James 1:5.

Once you've identified the what, start to ask God for the when, why, and how. He didn't bless you with talents and abilities for no reason, and the United States is very important to God. Utilizing the gifts God gave you only makes sense; however, augmenting those gifts by developing skills in areas where you are less gifted may be required in order to be all God wants you to be. It's easy to be a big fish in a small pond, but God wants so much more for your life. Reshaping America will be a daunting task, and in order to be up for the challenge, we can't rest on our laurels.

The time for simply mailing it in is over. The stakes are too high. To turn this ship around, we need all hands on deck! Besides, whenever God calls us to step up our game, a really cool thing happens: we get closer to Him. This country will never be reshaped unless its citizens rise up and do things that are impossible on our own but possible with the help of God.

Stepping out of our comfort zones and answering to a higher calling will accomplish two very important things. First, the country will be transformed and will start to resemble the great land that it once was. Second, and more importantly, God will get the glory. When we are willing to accept God's challenge to do extraordinary things, He will always help us do those things. When underqualified people are put in situations that they have no business being in and they succeed, God is glorified! Believers are encouraged to take on daunting tasks and non-believers are suddenly intrigued by the accomplishments of relatively unassuming people, thereby drawing them closer to a relationship with Jesus Christ.

The Bible is replete with stories of God choosing the most unlikely characters and charging them with extraordinary tasks. Joseph was cast into slavery by his own brothers; falsely accused of a crime, he rose to the second-highest position in all of Egypt! David was a lowly shepherd boy who, against all odds, fearlessly slew the mighty Goliath! Moses, who was slated to be killed as an infant, overcame countless obstacles en route to leading his people out of Egyptian bondage and into freedom! Mary, a young virgin from lowly Nazareth, the mother of the promised Messiah, declared in Luke 1:48 *"For He has been mindful of the humble state of His servant. From now on all generations will call me blessed."* The disciples themselves, who were largely uneducated and with no formal theological training, became some of the first tools to further the kingdom of God. It would have been illogical for Jesus Himself to leave the furtherance of his kingdom to these guys, but He did. The old adage is true: "God doesn't call the equipped, He equips the called."

Our problem is that we neglect to remember that the pedigrees of most great men and women of the Bible were quite ordinary. With this in mind, we should not let the fact that many of us are unremarkable be a reason to refuse to do big things for God. When I was growing up, I always looked forward to gym class. Despite being painfully skinny, I was a fast runner and a good athlete. However, there were some kids who not only didn't look forward to gym, they dreaded it. On the days we played basketball, football, or kickball, our gym teacher would select two captains, one for each team who stood in front of the class and selected kids to be on their teams. Typically, these kids were muscular, athletic, good looking, popular, you get the picture. Logically, their goal was to assemble the strongest, fastest, and most proficient athletes from the group in order to vanquish the other team. As you might imagine, the selection process was agonizingly slow, particularly for the kids who possessed none of those attributes.

As I said, I was a good athlete, but I was so skinny that I often got picked on because of it. So I sort of had one foot in each world. Usually I was either a captain or was selected as a player very early in the process. Other kids were not so fortunate. As the pile of little fourth-grade boys started to dwindle, the tension grew. The captains would look at each other and snicker at the dregs who hadn't yet been chosen.

I was a little more sensitive than most fourth graders, and this ritual affected me greatly. As the process unfolded, this amalgamation of undesirables oftentimes wicked together for support in a little ball as the pickens got slim. These precious children comprised the fat and the thin, the smelly and the uncool, the poor and the dim. Sometimes, but unfortunately not always, the gym teacher would mercifully put a halt to this public humiliation by finally dividing the last few kids up and assigning them to a particular team.

I'm no better than any of those captains, but when I got a chance to compile my team, I sometimes shook it up a bit. Don't get me wrong, I wanted to win the fourth period gym class basketball game as much as anyone else, but I also had a heart for the aforementioned undesirables. After a few logical selections of top-flight athletes, I selected one of the kids who normally got picked at the end of the process. You should have seen the looks on the faces of everyone in the gym. The coach could never quite figure out what I was doing.

The "it" kids would look at me and say, "What are you doing? Mike stinks!" or "That's pretty funny." Sadly, the most perplexed individuals in the room were those "undesirable" kids I selected.

Their opinion of themselves was largely the same as that of their peers. They kinda smiled at me as they sheepishly walked up to the front of the gym not really knowing what to make of all this. They must have thought, "What is this guy thinking? Doesn't he realize who I am? Doesn't he know I can't pull this off?"

Unfortunately, the thoughts that go through our minds and the minds of those around us are very much the same today when God calls us to do something that doesn't make sense to us. It is perfectly normal to feel scared, inadequate, and ill-equipped when God puts a daunting task before us. However, when the stakes are as high as they are in our country right now, it is not an option to just sink back into mediocrity. God loves this country and we should feel honored that He chooses unassuming individuals to turn it around. When God wants to evoke big change in the world he often uses little people to do it. The template I used for selecting certain kids back in fourth-grade gym class may not have made a whole lot of sense, but it is precisely the template God uses to further His kingdom.

Finally, despite the fact that our country has become unmoored from its biblical dock, we have reason to be hopeful. Actually, things are not as bad as they seem. There are countless times in the history of mankind where God's children declared, "This is it, it's over!" On a personal level, we often think that our lives are filled with more bad days than good ones. When something bad happens, we feel panicked, overwhelmed, scared, angry, and bitter, often toward God. We have no trouble remembering the circumstances we endured. But one of the reasons it *seems* there are many more rainy days than sunny ones is because of our lack of gratitude and attitude of entitlement.

We are often oblivious to God's blessings, yet we remember the truly bad times in our lives without even trying. The good or blessed days are not as easy to remember because they don't really seem like good days. Likewise, we are still the most blessed nation in all of history even if it doesn't always seem like it. Our unawareness of what a poor life 80% of the world endures contributes to our ingratitude for all God has done for us. If we took the time to compare our lifestyles to those of someone in any third-world country, we would be ashamed that we complain so much.

Oddly enough, many takers and producers in this country share one thing in common: they both have a sense of entitlement. The taker, because he feels he gets a raw deal and *someone's* gonna pay, and the producer because, "Hey, this is America, I should be able to have anything I want just because I'm an American!" It's hard to be truly grateful with either of these mindsets. Once we become more grateful for every blessing, it becomes easier to see how many good days God graciously gives us.

This attitude of gratitude prepares for this fight in two ways. First, once we accurately assess how blessed our lives are personally and how blessed we are as a nation, the mountain doesn't seem as high. The task, although daunting, is winnable. Second, a proper understanding of how much God has blessed us gives us a deeper understanding of His love for us. Although His love for the people of all nations is equal, American is something unique.

This unbridled blessing has, in my opinion, been bestowed upon us because our Constitution is predicated on Judeo-Christian principles and our historical obedience to these sacred beliefs. Obedience to God and how that obedience corresponds to His blessing is nothing new. The Jewish people have a very long and predictable history of blessings and curses that directly correlate with their willingness to obey or disobey the God of Israel. The US is no different.

Prayer

I urge, then, first of all, that petitions, prayers, intercession and thanksgiving be made for all people—for kings and all those in authority, that we may live peaceful and quiet lives in all godliness and holiness. This is good, and pleases God our Savior.

—1 Timothy 2:1-3

If we are going to pull this off, we need to pray. Revelation 3:15-16 says: "I know your deeds, you are neither cold nor hot. I wish you were either one or the other! So, because you are lukewarm—neither hot nor cold—I am about to spit you out of my mouth." These verses are an admonishment of the church in Laodicea which had become complacent and lukewarm. They really didn't stand for anything. They were basically mailing it in. Sound familiar? God doesn't want us to go through the motions in our Christian walk. We should pray for our leaders, our fellow citizens, our families, our vocation, and everything in between.

Prayer changes things. Psalm 34:14-15 says, *"Turn from evil and do good; seek peace and pursue it. The eyes of the Lord are on the righteous, and his ears are attentive to their cry."* Are you crying out to the Lord with concerns for our country? Remember the lady in my wife's bible study who didn't pay attention to the war in Iraq because it was too upsetting? Well, how is anyone going to know what to pray for if they don't know what ills afflict this nation? We should have the mind of Christ. How do we get this? We already have it. 1 Corinthians 2:16 says, *"Who has the mind of the Lord so as to instruct him? But we have the mind of Christ."* We need only to listen to that still small voice called the Holy Spirit in order to know what God thinks about the problems facing this nation.

RESHAPING AMERICA

Once we hear from the Holy Spirit, we will be burdened to pray for the things that trouble Him. Matthew 7:7 tells us *"Ask and it will be given to you; seek and you will find; knock and the door will be opened to you."* God wants to bless us, but He is waiting for us to petition Him. In these critical times, ignorance and apathy are not an option. We should ask God to turn this nation around now!

Our prayers are kind of like our checkbooks; they reflect what is important to us. Our checkbook chronicles the things we find important enough to spend money on. Similarly, what we pray for reflects our most important needs and wants. Shouldn't everyone want our nation to be great? How much time do we actually spend praying for it? What's actually more troubling than the aforementioned category of citizens are individuals who do pray quite fervently for God to intervene and put the brakes on our country's current skid. Yes these individuals are keenly attuned to a wide array of cultural problems, but are they *genuinely* praying for the hearts of our leaders and fellow citizens to change? Love of country is great but love of our fellow man is even greater. 1 John 4:11-12 says, *"Dear friends, since God so loved us, we also ought to love one another. No one has ever seen God; but if we love one another, God lives in us and his love is made complete in us."* Do you love Barack Obama? How about George W. Bush, Mitt Romney, Hillary or Bill Clinton? How fervently do we pray for our leaders to have a true change of heart and start legislating and governing with God at the core of all their decisions? Do we just pray for our favorite politicians to stop our least favorite ones? Although we should pray for Godly men and women to be a legislative firewall on the behalf of good, do we devote equal time petitioning the Lord to change the hearts of our political adversaries? Or do we skip praying for them because of our *own* hate-filled souls? Or maybe we think they're lost causes.

Let's look at 2 Chronicles 33:10-13:

The Lord spoke to Manasseh and his people, but they paid no attention. So the Lord brought against them the army commanders of the king of Assyria, who took Manasseh prisoner, put a hook in his nose, bound him with bronze shackles and took him to Babylon. In his distress he sought the favor of the Lord his God and humbled himself greatly before the God of his ancestors. And when he prayed to Him, the Lord was moved by his entreaty and listened to his plea; so he brought him back to Jerusalem and to his kingdom. Then Manasseh knew that the Lord is God.

There's hope for even the most corrupt politicians that serve us as Proverbs 21:1 tells us: "In the Lord's hand the king's heart is a stream of water that he channels toward all who please him." It may seem like this big blue marble is spinning out of control, but God has us in the palm of His hand. God is not surprised by the evil things people do to take this world off course. Even though I urge you to do your part, we must ultimately trust in Him to put this great land of ours back on course, and I believe He will.

Well, you've read the book. I've done my job. It's your turn. Rest assured, Satan will try to snuff out any education, motivation, or inspiration that you've derived from these pages. It's critical that you keep looking upward every day as Satan thinks this country's demise is at hand. He knows you're busy, tired, fearful, and it's all you can do to keep your own family's ship afloat. Be forewarned, when you commit to reshape this country for the better he will bring out the big guns. You know this is not going to be easy and you don't care. YOU are different. You know that anything worth fighting for—your family, your community, the soul of our nation—doesn't come easily. By now you've decided, as I did years ago, *I'm in!* I'm proud of you, your family and friends are proud of you, and most importantly, our heavenly Father is beaming about the decision you've made!

Now go out and reshape America!

ACTION STEPS

1. Ask yourself: Will this country really be okay without God's blessing?

2. Research the history of other countries/cultures before us. How are they doing today? Do they even exist? If not, why?

3. Ask yourself: What am I doing to help my country return to greatness?

4. Ask God to help you have a heart for this nation. Ask Him to reveal to you what your part is in bringing this country back to its biblical roots.

5. Pray for this nation! Pray for our president, the judiciary, Congress, our churches, and our fellow countrymen to live with God's ways in mind at every turn.

6. Receive God's guidance and help so you can reshape America!

Endnotes

1. Meghan, Georgia Congressional Candidate: Russia/ Ukraine conflict could be become an 'international catastrophe' glennbeck.com 7/18/2014, Accessed 11/10/15.

2. David Barton, "Were All of America's Founding Fathers Racist, Pro-slavery, and Hypocrites? Founding Fathers and Slavery, 1999.

3. Ibid

4. "In Circumstances as Dark as These…" Founders Quotes.

5. "Founders Online: From James Madison to James Monroe, 5 October 1786," Archives.gov.

6. "John Adams' Diary," Constitution.org

7. "Thomas Jefferson," Voices of Freedom.

8. Mary Fairchild, "Spiritual Quotes of the Founding Fathers (Page 3)," About Christianity.

9. "Faith of Our Fathers," Alexander Hamilton.

10. "Faith of Our Fathers," Patrick Henry.

11. "Party of 1776 – United States Founding Fathers – John Witherspoon – Quotes," Party of 1776.

12. "Samuel Adams Quotes from 1780 to the End of His Life," Revolutionary War and Beyond.

13. "United States Founding Fathers: Roger Sherman," Party of 1776.

14. Daniel Dreisbach, "The Mythical 'Wall of Separation': How a Misguided Metaphor Changed Church-State Law, Policy, and Discourse," The Heritage Foundation, 2006.

15. Terence P. Jeffery, "Newseum: Only 19% Know First Amendment Guarantees Freedom of religion", Cnsnews.com, 2015.

16. Michael Gryboski, "Houston Mayor Annise Parker Drops Subpoenas Demanding Pastors Turn Over Their Sermons", Christian Post.

17. "Adolf Hitler Hated Christianity," Adolph Hitler Hated Christianity.

18. Ibid.

19. "Adherents.com," The Religion of Joseph Stalin, Communist Leader.

20. "Communism Persecutes Religion," No Communism, Communism Persecutes Religion.

21. Andrew Thomas, "In Their Own Words: Lenin, Stalin, Obama, and Hillary," American Thinker, 2014.

22. "Excerpts from President's Speech to National Association of Evangelicals," The New York Times, March 8, 1983.

23. Richard Lee, *The American Patriot's Bible: The Word of God and the Shaping of America*, "Nashville, Tennessee: Thomas Nelson, 2009, 774.

24. Ibid., 298.

25. American Heritage Dictionary, 3rd Edition

26. "Exemption Requirements 501(c)(3) Organizations," Internal Revenue Service, January 13, 2015.

27. "Types of Organizations Exempt Under Section 501(c)(4)," Internal Revenue Service, June 13, 2014.

28. Wallsten, Peter, Bauerlein, 4/29/10. "Crist Looks To Go It Alone', The Wall Street Journal

    Cave, Damien and Fineout, Gary 5/12/2009, "Restless in Tallahassee" New York Times

    "Former Florida Governor Charlie Crist Attacks Rivals in New Book," WTSP. Accessed 11/14/15.

    Sullivan, Sean, "Hillary Clinton to Campaign for Charlie Crist," Washington Post 9/23/14. Accessed 11/10/15

Johnson, Andrew, In 1998 Charlie Crist called for Bill Clinton Resignation, Now He's Welcoming His Endorsement, National Review, 9/2/14   accessed 11/10/15

29. "Your Vote Matters," The Providence Forum, June 13, 2014.

30. T. Jefferson, "What is 'Social Justice'?" Glenn Beck, March 24, 2010.

31. Bill Koenig, "Sharing the Gospel: A Gathering Interview With Franklin Graham," The Gathering RSS, November 29, 2009.

32. "Revolution of Social Justice," Tony Campolo, April 30, 2010.

33. Warren W. Wiersbe, sermon quotes.com accessed on 11/10/15.

34. Kelsey Dallas, "Hillary Clinton Praises Bible, Methodist Upbringing," Deseret News, June 24, 2014.

35. thefreedictionary.com. Accessed 11/10/15

36. Phillip Pullella, "U.N. Should Encourage Redistribution of Wealth, Pope Says," Reuters UK, May 9, 2014.

37. "Pope Leo XIII 28 December 1878 on Socialism," Eternal Word Television Network.

38. Ibid.

39. Kerry Picket, 2015, "Hillary On Abortion: 'Deep-Seated Cultural Codes, Religious Beliefs And Structural Biases Have To Be Changed,'" *The Daily Caller.*

40. RCRC.org homepage – policy/access-to-abortion care 9/14/2015.

41. Scott Douglas Gerber, "Clarence Thomas, gay marriage and The Declaration of Independence." Washington Examiner, 2015.

42. Fox News, 'Threat to Democracy': see the 4 Justices' Dissent on Gay Marriage Ruling. 2015.

43. Antonin Scalia, 2015, 'Warning to America in Dissent"Tulsatoday.Com.

44. NBC Nightly News, 'Outed In Mom's Obituary, Teacher Says She was Fired' April 27, 2013

45. Elisha Fieldstadt and Tracy Connor, Pope Urges Spreading 'Little Signs Of Love' During Last U.S. Mass In Philadelphia. NBCnews.com April 28, 2015

46. John Greenberg and Molly Moorhead, Politifacts Guide to Mitt Romney and abortion. politifact.com 10/19/12. Accessed 8/17/15

47. Steven Ertelt, Gallup Poll – 58% of Americans Oppose All Or Most Abortion, lifenews.com 5/10/13. Accessed 7/21/15.

48. Dave Warner, "Prosecution Rests in Philadelphia Abortion Doctor Trial," Reuters, April 18, 2013.

49. Matt Walsh, "Black Lives Matter, So It's Times To Outlaw Abortion," The Blaze, November 26, 2014.

50. Lifenews, "7 Incredibly Shocking Quotes From Planned Parenthood Founder Margaret Sanger" 2015.

51. James MacPherson, "North Dakota Gov. Jack Dalrymple Approves 6-week Abortion Ban," Washington Times, March 26, 2013.

52. Jill Stanek, 'Obamas Record on The Born Alive Infant Protection Act', jillstanek.com accessed 5/13/15.

53. Jill Stanek, "Top 10 Reasons Obama Voted Against The Illinois Born-Alive Infants Protection Act," Illinois Review.

54. Fox News, "Federal Judge Rules Morning-After Pill Must Be Available for Women of All Ages," 2013.

55. Billy Hallowell, 2014, "Shock Report: Aborted and Miscarried Babies were Incinerated And Used To Heat U.K. Hospitals," *The Blaze*.

56. Billy Hallowell, 2014, "'I Am Horrified': Politicians Take Swift Action After Discovering That Fetal Remains Were Possibly Used To Generate Energy," *The Blaze*.

57. Steven Ertelt, 'Historic Symposium Focuses on Opposing Assisted Suicide' 12/9/07.

58. Susan Harding, 2015, "Letter Noting Assisted Suicide Raises Questions," *KATU.Com*.

59. Steven Ertelt, 2015, "House Votes To Repeal IPAB, Obamacare 'Death Panels,'" *LifeNews.Com*.

60. Department of Homeland Security – 'Estimates of Unauthorized Immigrant Population Residing in the United States. Accessed 11/10/15.

61. K. Scott Schaeffer, "Greed and Oppression of the Poor," *Christian Left Blog*, January 4, 2014.

62. Rasmussen Reports, 'Voters Want To Build a Wall, Deport Felon Illegal Immigrants. 8/19/15. Accessed 11/10/15.

63. Fred Barbash, 2015, "Federal Judge in Texas Blocks Obama Immigration Orders," *Washington Post*.

64. Ronald Reagan, 2015, "Ronald Reagan Quotes At Brainyquote.com," *Brainyquote*.

65. Alexander Tytler, 2015, "Alexander Fraser Tytler Quotes," *Goodreads*.

66. Walter Jones, 2013, "Study: Welfare Programs Discourage Work, Marriage," *Online Athens*.

67. Tim McMahon, unemploymentdata.com, Current Unemployment Rate is 9.5% (BLS) or 13.8% (Gallup), 11/6/15. Accessed 11/10/15.

68. Dave Urbanski, 2015, 'Greece Enters Uncharted Territory After Voters Overwhelmingly Reject Austerity Measures', *The Blaze*.

69. David Shaywitz, 2013, "Five Take-Aways from Whole Foods CEO John Mackey's Surprising New Book," *Forbes*.

70. Jeff Kearns, 2014, "David Brat Sees Virtue as Foundation of U.S. Economic Gains," *Bloomberg.com*.

71. Ibid.

72. Phillip Klein, 2009, "The Myth of the 46 Million," *The American Spectator.*

73. Drew Griffin, 2014, "Inside CNN's Investigation: Fear Kept the VA Scandal A Secret - Cnnpolitics.Com," *CNN.*

74. Congress.gov, 2015, "s.142 – 113th Congress (2013-2014): Hyde Amendment Codification Act," *Library of Congress.*

75. Bridget Johnson, 2010, "Stupak Stripped of 'Defender of Life' Award He Was to receive This Week," *TheHill. com.*

76. Mark Blanton, 2014, "Law Professor Discusses Hobby Lobby Case at Cape Church," *Semissourian.com.*

77. Jose Delreal, 2015, "ObamaCare Consultant Under Fire for 'Stupidity of the American Voter' Comment," *Washington Post.*

78. Jim Wallis, *God's Politics,* page 236.

79. "SCOTUS Announces Review of CEI's Healthcare Case: King vs. Burwell," Competitive Enterprise Institute. 11/7/2014.

80. Chris Field, 2015, "The top 15 Antonin Scalia Quotes From His New Obamacare Dissent, the Blaze.

81. Ted Cruz, 2015, 'Constitutional remedies to a Lawless Supreme Court, Nationalreview.Com.

82. Alex Murashko, 2014, "Author Debunks Myths about Divorce Rates, Including of Churchgoers," *Christian Post.*

83. John Glubb, *The Fate of Empires and the Search For Survival*, 1/1/78.

84. Roger Clegg, 'Latest Statistics on Out of Wedlock Births', National Review 10/11/13. Accessed 11/12/15.

85. Charles Stanley, Life Principle 2 – 'A life of Obedience,' sermon, 7/2/14.

86. Madeleine Morgenstern, 2013, "Melissa Harris-Perry: 'I Stand By 'Kids Belong to Whole Communities''' 'MSNBC Promo," *The Blaze.*

87. Ibid.

88. Brownie Marie, 2014, "Colorado 10-Year-Old Fourth-Graders Busted For Selling Marijuana At School," Christian News on Christian Today, *Christiantoday.Com.*

89. bid.

90. Pat Loeb, 2015, "20 Students Taken To Hospital After First Grader Brings Heroin to Cobbs Creek School," *Philadelphia.Cbslocal.Com.*

91. Maggie Avants, 2014, "Attorney: Temecula Teacher Stops 1st-Grader From Talking About Jesus in School, *Temecula, California Patch.*

92. Billy Hallowell, 2013, "Teacher Admits She 'Prayed Out Loud' During Violent Tornado: 'I Did The Teacher Thing That We're Probably Not Supposed To Do,'" *The Blaze.*

93. Sol Alinsky, "Playboy Interview: Saul Alinsky," March 1972.

94. Ravi Zacharias, position paper entitled: *Reaching the "Happy thinking pagan"* 10/1/95. Accessed from the RZIM website 11/12/15.

95. StudyLight.org, 2015, "Vine's Expository Dictionary."

96. *Monumental*. 2012. DVD. Pyro Pictures.

97. Ibid.

Bibliography

113ᵗʰ Congress. "S.142 – 113th Congress (2013-2014): Hyde Amendment Codification Act." *United States Congress.* January 24, 2013. https://www.congress.gov/bill/113th-congress/senate-bill/142/text.

Adams, John. "John Adams' Diary." Constitution Society. Accessed May 12, 2015. http://www.Constitution.org/primary-sources/adamsdiary.html.

Adams, Samuel. "Samuel Adams Quotes from 1780 to the End of His Life." *Revolutionary War and Beyond.* Accessed May 12, 2015. http://www.Revolutionary-War-And-Beyond.com/samuel-adams-quotes-3.html.

Adherents.com. "The Religion of Joseph Stalin, Communist Leader." *Adherents.com.* Accessed May 12, 2015. http://www.Adherents.com/people/ps/Joseph_Stalin.html.

Adolph Hitler Hated Christianity. "Adolph Hitler Hated Christianity." *Adolph Hitler Hated Christianity.* October 6, 2011. http://HitlerNoChristian.Blogspot.com/.

Alinsky, Saul. "Playboy Interview: Saul Alinsky." *Playboy,* March 1972.

The American Heritage Dictionary of the English Language, Third Edition. Boston: Houghton Mifflin Company, 1992.

Associated Press. "Excerpts From President's Speech to National Association of Evangelicals." *The New York Times,* March 8, 1983.

Avants, Maggie. "Attorney: Temecula Teacher Stops 1st-Grader From Talking About Jesus In School." *Temecula Patch* (Temecula, CA), January 14, 2014.

Barbash, Fred "Federal Judge in Texas Blocks Obama Immigration Orders." *Washington Post,* February 17, 2015.

Barker, Kenneth L, and Donald W. Burdick. *Zondervan NIV Study Bible.* Grand Rapids, MI: Zondervan, 2002.

Barton, David. "Were All of America's Founding Fathers Racist, Pro-slavery, and Hypocrites?" *ChristianAnswers.net.* Accessed May 12, 2015. http://christiananswers.net/q-wall/wal-g003.html.

Blanton, Mark. "Law Professor Discusses Hobby Lobby Case at Cape Church." *Southeast Missourian* (Cape Girardeau, MO), June 1, 2014.

Campolo, Tony. "Revolution of Social Justice." *Tony Campolo.* April 30, 2010. http://TonyCampolo.org/wp-content/

uploads/sermons/04302010-Walla-Walla-University-Forum.doc.

Cave, Damien and Gary Fineout. " Restless in Tallahassee, or With Eye on 2012, Governor Rolls Dice." *The New York Times.* May 12, 2009. http://www.NYTimes.com/2009/05/13/us/13cristq.html?_r=0.

Clegg, Roger. "Latest Statistics on Out-of-Wedlock Births." *National Review.* October 11, 2013. http://www.National-Review.com/corner/360990/latest-statistics-out-wedlock-births-roger-clegg.

Competitive Enterprise Institute. "SCOTUS Announces Review of CEI's Healthcare Case: King v. Burwell." *Competitive Enterprise Institute.* November 7, 2014. https://CEI.org/content/scotus-announces-review-cei%E2%80%99s-healthcare-case-king-v-burwell.

Cox, Ramsey. "Corker Blocks Paul's Bill to End Aid to Palestinian Authority." *The Hill.* July 7, 2014. http://thehill.com/blogs/floor-action/senate/211496-corker-blocks-pauls-bill-to-end-aid-to-palestinian-authority.

Cruz, Ted. "Constitutional Remedies to a Lawless Supreme Court." *National Review.* June 26, 2015. http://www.NationalReview.com/article/420409/constitutional-remedies-lawless-supreme-court-ted-cruz.

Dallas, Kelsey. "Hillary Clinton Praises Bible, Methodist Upbringing." *Deseret News* (Salt Lake City, UT), June 24, 2014.

DelReal, Jose. "Obamacare Consultant Under Fire For 'Stupidity of the American Voter' Comment." *Washington Post*, November 11, 2014.

Dreisbach, Daniel L. "The Mythical 'Wall of Separation': How a Misused Metaphor Changed Church–State Law, Policy, and Discourse." *The Heritage Foundation.* Accessed May 12, 2015. http://www.Heritage.org/research/reports/2006/06/the-mythical-wall-of-separation-how-a-misused-metaphor-changed-church-state-law-policy-and-discourse.

Ertelt, Steven. "Gallup Poll: 58% of Americans Oppose All of Most Abortions." *LifeNews.com.* May 10, 2013. http://www.LifeNews.com/2013/05/10/gallup-poll-58-of-americans-oppose-all-or-most-abortions/.

"Historic Symposium Focuses on Opposing Assisted Suicide and Euthanasia." *LifeNews.com.* December 9, 2007. http://www.LifeNews.com/2007/12/09/bio-2289/.

"House Votes To Repeal Independent Payment Advisory Board (IPAB), Obamacare 'Death Panels.'" *LifeNews.Com.* June 24, 2015. http://www.LifeNews.com/2015/06/24/house-votes-to-repeal-independent-payment-advisory-board-ipab-obamacares-death-panels/.

Fairchild, Mary. "Christian Quotes of the Founding Fathers." *about religion.* Accessed May 12, 2015. http://christianity.about.com/od/independenceday/a/foundingfathers.htm.

Faith of Our Fathers. "Alexander Hamilton." *Faith of Our Fathers.* Accessed May 12, 2015. http://FaithOfOurFathers.net/"-Patrick Henry." *Faith of Our Fathers.* Accessed May 12, 2015. http://FaithOfOurFathers.net/patrick-henry.html.

Farlex. "Envy." *The Free Dictionary.* Accessed November 10, 2015. http://www.TheFreeDictionary.com/envy.

Field, Chris. "The Top 15 Antonin Scalia Quotes From His New Obamacare Dissent." *The Blaze,* June 25, 2015. http://

www.TheBlaze.com/stories/2015/06/25/the-top-15-quotes-from-justice-scalias-dissent-in-king-v-burwell/.

FoxNews.com. "Federal Judge Rules Morning-After Pill Must Be Available for Women of All Ages." *FoxNews.com.* April 5, 2013. http://www.FoxNews.com/politics/2013/04/05/federal-judge-rules-morning-after-abortion-pill-must-be-available-for-women-all.html.

Fox News Insider. "'Threat to Democracy': See the 4 Justices' Dissent on Gay Marriage Ruling." Fox News Insider. June 26, 2015. http://insider.foxnews.com/2015/06/26/quotes-scalia-thomas-roberts-alito-dissent-supreme-court-gay-marriage-ruling.

"George Washington." *George Washington.* Accessed May 12, 2015.

Gerber, Scott Douglas. "Clarence Thomas, Gay Marriage and the Declaration of Independence." *Washington Examiner.* July 3, 2015. http://www.washingtonexaminer.com/clarence-thomas-gay-marriage-and-the-declaration-of-independence/article/2567372.

Glubb, John. *The Fate of Empires and the Search for Survival.* Edinburgh: Blackwood, 1978.

Greenberg, Jon and Molly Moorhead. "PolitiFact's Guide to Mitt Romney and Abortion." *PolitiFact.* October 19, 2012. http://www.PolitiFact.com/truth-o-meter/article/2012/oct/19/politifacts-guide-mitt-romney-and-abortion/.

Griffin, Drew, Scott Bronstein, and Nelli Black. "Fear Kept the VA Scandal a Secret." *CNN.* June 5, 2014. http://www.CNN.com/2014/06/05/politics/va-scandal-fear-secret/.

Gryboski, Michael. "Houston Mayor Annise Parker Drops Subpoenas Demanding Pastors Turn Over Their Sermons." *Christian Post.* October 29, 2014. http://www.Christian Post.com/news/mayor-annise-parker-drops-subpoenas-against-houston-pastors-128816/.

Hale, Tabitha. "Stupak: HHS Mandate Violates My Obamacare Compromise." *Breitbart.* September 4, 2012. http://www. Breitbart.com/big-government/2012/09/04/stupak-president-played-me-with-obamacare-deal/.

Hallowell, Billy. "'I Am Horrified': Politicians Take Swift Action After Discovering That Fetal Remains Were Possibly Used to Generate Energy." *The Blaze.* April 24, 2014. http://www. TheBlaze.com/stories/2014/04/24/i-am-horrified-politicians-take-swift-action-after-discovering-that-fetal-remains-were-possibly-used-to-generate-energy/.

"Shock Report: Aborted and Miscarried Babies Were Incinerated and Used to Heat U.K. Hospitals." *The Blaze.* March 24, 2014. http://www.TheBlaze.com/stories/2014/03/24/shock-report-aborted-and-miscarried-babies-were-incinerated-and-used-to-heat-u-k-hospitals/.

"Teacher Admits She 'Prayed Out Loud' During Violent Tornado: 'I Did The Teacher Thing That We're Probably Not Supposed to Do.'" *The Blaze.* May 22, 2013. http://www. TheBlaze.com/stories/2013/05/22/teacher-admits-she-prayed-out-loud-during-violent-tornado-i-did-the-teacher-thing-that-were-probably-not-supposed-to-do/.

Hancock, John. "In Circumstances as Dark as These, It Becomes Us, as Men and Christians…" *Founders Quotes.* Accessed May 12, 2015. http://FoundersQuotes.com/founding-fathers-quote/in-circumstances-as-dark-as-these-it-be-comes-us-as-men-and-christians/.

Harding, Susan. "Letter Noting Assisted Suicide Raises Questions. *KATU 2.* November 20, 2008. http://www.KATU.com/news/26119539.html.

Internal Revenue Service. "Exemption Requirements 501(c)(3) Organizations." *Internal Revenue Service.* January 8, 2015. https://www.IRS.gov/Charities-&-Non-Profits/Charitable-Organizations/Exemption-Requirements-Section-501(c)(3)-Organizations.

Internal Revenue Service. "Types of Organizations Exempt under Section 501(c)(4)." *Internal Revenue Service.* January 13, 2015. https://www.IRS.gov/Charities-&-Non-Profits/Other-Non-Profits/Types-of-Organizations-Exempt-under-Section-501(c)(4).

Jefferson, T. "Glenn Beck: What Is 'Social Justice'?" *Glenn Beck.* March 24, 2010. http://www.GlennBeck.com/content/articles/article/198/38320/.

Jefferson, Thomas. "Thomas Jefferson." *Voices of Freedom.* Accessed May 12, 2015. http://www.VoicesOfFreedom.us/voices/thomasjefferson/thomasjefferson7.htm.

Jeffrey, Terence P. "Newseum: Only 19% Know First Amendment Guarantees Freedom of Religion." *cnsnews.com.* July 6, 2015. http://www.cnsnews.com/news/article/terence-p-jeffrey/newseum-only-19-know-1st-amendment-guarantees-freedom-religion.

Johnson, Andrew. "In 1998, Charlie Crist Called for Bill Clinton's Resignation, Now He's Welcoming His Endorsement." *National Review.* September 2, 2014. http://www.National-

Review.com/corner/386880/1998-charlie-crist-called-bill-clintons-resignation-now-hes-welcoming-his-endorsement

Johnson, Bridget. "Stupak Stripped of 'Defender of Life' Award He Was to Receive This Week." *The Hill.* March 22, 2010. http://TheHill.com/blogs/blog-briefing-room/news/88215-stupak-stripped-of-defender-of-life-award-he-was-to-receive-this-week.

Jones, Walter C. "Study: Welfare Programs Discourage Work, Marriage." *Athens Banner-Herald* (Athens, GA). *March 13, 2013.* http://OnlineAthens.com/local-news/2013-03-13/study-welfare-programs-discourage-work-marriage.

Kearns, Jeff. "David Brat Sees Virtue As Foundation Of U.S. Economic Gains." *BloombergBusiness.* June 11, 2014. http://www.Bloomberg.com/news/articles/2014-06-11/david-brat-sees-virtue-as-foundation-of-u-s-economic-success.

Klein, Philip. "The Myth of the 46 Million." *The American Spectator.* March 20, 2009.

Koenig, Bill. "Sharing the Gospel: A Gathering Interview with Franklin Graham." *The Gathering.* October 6, 2009. http://TheGathering.com/e-updates/sharing-the-gospel-a-gathering-interview-with-franklin-graham/.

Lee, Richard. *The American Patriot's Bible: The Word of God and the Shaping of America.* Nashville, TN: Thomas Nelson, 2009.

Loeb, Pat and Walt Hunter. "20 Students Taken to Hospital After First Grader Brings Heroin to Cobbs Creek School." *CBS Philly.* June 10, 2014. http://Philadelphia. CBSLocal.com/2014/06/10/drug-scare-at-a-west-phila-school-when-first-grader-brings-in-unknown-packets/.

MacPherson, James. "North Dakota Gov. Jack Dalrymple Approves 6-week Abortion Ban." *Washington Times*. March 26, 2013. http://www.WashingtonTimes.com/news/2013/mar/26/ north-dakota-gov-jack-dalrymple-approves-6-week-ab/.

Madison, James. "From James Madison to James Monroe, 5 October 1786." *Founders Online*. Accessed May 12, 2015. http://Founders.Archives.gov/documents/Madison/ 01-09-02-0054

Marie, Brownie. "Colorado 10-Year-Old Fourth-Graders Busted for Selling Marijuana at School" *Christian Today.* April 25, 2014. http://www.ChristianToday.com/article/colorado.10.year.old.fourth.graders.busted.selling.marijuana. school/37032.htm.

McMahon, Tim. "Current U-6 Unemployment Rate." *UnemploymentData.com*. Accessed November 10, 2015. http://unemploymentdata.com/current-u6-unemployment-rate/.

Meghan. "Georgia Congressional Candidate: Russia/Ukraine Conflict Could Become an 'International Catastrophe.' *Glenn Beck.* July 18, 2014. http://www.GlennBeck. com/2014/07/18/georgia-congressional-candidate-russiaukraine-conflict-could-become-an-international-catastrophe/.

Monumental: In Search of America's National Treasure. Directed by Duane Barnhart. 2012. DVD. Oklahoma City, OK: Pyro Pictures, 2012. DVD.

Morgenstern, Madeleine. "Melissa Harris-Perry: 'I Stand By' 'Kids Belong To Whole Communities' MSNBC Promo." *The Blaze.* April 13, 2013. http://www.TheBlaze.com/stories/2013/04/13/melissa-harris-perry-i-stand-by-kids-be-long-to-whole-communities-msnbc-promo/.

Murashko, Alex. "Author Debunks Myths About Divorce Rates, Including of Churchgoers." *Christian Post.* May 16, 2014. http://www.ChristianPost.com/news/author-de-bunks-myths-about-divorce-rates-including-of-churchgo-ers-119843/.

NoCommunism.com. "Communism Persecutes Religion." *NoCommunism.com.* Accessed May 12, 2015. http://www.nocommunism.com/communism-and-big-government-articles/communism-persecutes-religion/.

"Party of 1776 - United States Founding Fathers - John Wither-spoon - Quotes." Party of 1776 - United States Founding Fathers - John Witherspoon - Quotes. Accessed May 12, 2015.

Picket, Kerry. "Hillary On Abortion: 'Deep-Seated Cultural Codes, Religious Beliefs and Structural Biases Have to Be Changed.'" *The Daily Caller.* April 23, 2015. http://dailycaller.com/2015/04/23/hillary-on-abortion-deep-seat-ed-cultural-codes-religious-beliefs-and-structural-biases-have-to-be-changed/.

Pope Leo XIII. *Quod Apostolici Muneris (On Socialism).* Rome: Vatican Press, 1878.

Providence Forum. "Your Vote Matters." The Providence Forum. June 13, 2014. http://www.ProvidenceForum.org/yourvo-tematters.

Pullella, Phillip. "U.N. Should Encourage Redistribution of Wealth, Pope Says." *Reuters.* May 9, 2014. http://www.Reuters.com/article/us-pope-un-idUSKBN0DP0WU20140509.

Rasmussen Reports. "Voters Want to Build a Wall, Deport Felon Illegal immigrants." *Rasmussen Reports.* August 19, 2015. http://www.RasmussenReports.com/public_content/politics/current_events/immigration/august_2015/voters_want_to_build_a_wall_deport_felon_illegal_immigrants.

Reagan, Ronald. "Ronald Reagan Quotes at BrainyQuote.Com." *BrainyQuote.* Accessed May 13, 2015. http://www.BrainyQuote.com/search_results.html?q=ronald+reagan.

Religious Coalition for Reproductive Choice. "Access to Abortion Care." *Religious Coalition for Reproductive Choice.* Accessed 9/14/2015. http://RCRC.org/homepage/policy/access-to-abortion-care/.

Scalia, Antonin. "Warning to America in Dissent." *Tulsa Today.* July 4, 2015. http://www.TulsaToday.com/2015/07/04/scalias-warning-to-america/.

Schaeffer, K. Scott. "Greed and Oppression of the Poor." *Christian Left Blog.* January 4, 2014. http://www.TheChristianLeftBlog.org/blog-home/greed-oppression-of-the-poor-by-k-scott-schaeffer.

Shaywitz, David. "Five Take-Aways from Whole Foods CEO John Mackey's Surprising New Book." *Forbes.* February 16, 2013. http://www.Forbes.com/sites/davidshaywitz/2013/02/16/five-take-aways-from-whole-foods-ceo-john-mackeys-surprising-new-book/.

Stanek, Jill. "Top 10 Reasons Obama Voted Against the Illinois Born-Alive Infants Protection Act." *Illinois Review.* January 10, 2008. http://IllinoisReview.typepad.com/illinoisreview/2008/01/top-10-reasons.html.

Stanley, Charles. "A Life of Obedience." *In Touch Ministries.* November 6, 2011. http://www.InTouch.org/watch/life-principles-to-live-by/a-life-of-obedience-video.

Sullivan, Sean. "Hillary Clinton to Campaign for Charlie Crist." *The Washington Post.* September 23, 2014. https://www.WashingtonPost.com/news/post-politics/wp/2014/09/23/hillary-clinton-to-campaign-for-charlie-crist-oct-2/.

Thomas, Andrew. "In Their Own Words: Lenin, Stalin, Obama, and Hillary." *American Thinker.* January 23, 2014. http://www.AmericanThinker.com/articles/2014/01/in_their_own_words_lenin_stalin_obama_and_hillary.html.

"United States Founding Fathers: Roger Sherman." *Party of 1776.* Accessed May 12, 2015.

Urbanski, Dave. "Greece Enters Uncharted Territory After Voters Overwhelmingly Reject Austerity Measures." *The Blaze.* July 5, 2015. http://www.TheBlaze.com/stories/2015/07/05/greece-enters-uncharted-territory-after-voters-overwhelmingly-reject-austerity-measures/.

U.S. Department of Homeland Security. "Estimates of the Unauthorized Immigrant Population Residing in the United States: January 2012." *U.S. Department of Homeland Security.* Accessed November 10, 2015. http://www.DHS.gov/publication/estimates-unauthorized-immigrant-population-residing-united-states-january-2012.

Vine, W.E. *Vine's Expository Dictionary.* Nashville, TN: Thomas Nelson, 2003.

Wallis, Jim. *God's Politics: Why the Right Gets It Wrong and the Left Doesn't Get It.* New York: HarperCollins, 2005.

Wallsten, Peter and Valerie Bauerlein. "Crist Looks to Go It Alone." *The Wall Street Journal.* Last updated April 29, 2010. http://www.WSJ.com/articles/SB1000142405274 87044235045752123203 10724084.

Walsh, Matt. "Black Lives Matter, So It's Time to Outlaw Abortion." *The Blaze.* November 26, 2014. http://www.theblaze.com/contributions/black-lives-matter-so-its-time-to-outlaw-abortion/.

Warner, Dave. "Prosecution Rests in Philadelphia Abortion Doctor Trial." *Reuters.* April 18, 2013. Accessed May 12, 2015. http://www.Reuters.com/article/us-usa-philadelphia-clinic-idUSBRE93H1D720130418.

Wiersbe, Warren W. "Warren W. Wiersbe." *SermonQuotes.com.* Accessed November 10, 2015. http://www.SermonQuotes.com/?s=wiersbe&submit=Search.

Yeh, Becky. "Seven Incredibly Shocking Quotes from Planned Parenthood Founder Margaret Sanger." LifeNews.com. February 23, 2015. http://www.LifeNews.com/2015/02/23/7-shocking-quotes-from-planned-parenthood-founder-margaret-sanger/.

Zacharias, Ravi. "Reaching the Happy Thinking Pagan." *Ravi Zacharias International Ministries.* October 1, 1995. http://RZIM.org/just-thinking/reaching-the-happy-thinking-pagan.

For more information on
Curt Flewelling
and his ministry go to:

www.reshapingamerica.org

To order more copies
of Reshaping America go to:

amazon.com

or

https://www.createspace.com/6090584

Made in the USA
Coppell, TX
08 October 2021

63715375R00128